SOUTH AMERICA: RIVER TRIPS

George N. Bradt

With Contributions by:

Richard Bangs
Marc Dubin
Penny & Russell Jennings
Jane Robinson
Robin Robinson
Joseph Rosenbloom III
Nick Ryalls
John Tichenor

Published by
Bradt Enterprises

54 Dudley Street
Cambridge,
Massachusetts
U.S.A. 02140

41 Nortoft Road
Chalfont St. Peter,
Bucks—SL9 0NA
ENGLAND

Dedicated to my
Grandmother: Alma Reed Bradt
with love and respect

Copyright © 1981
George N. Bradt

Reproduction of this book, in any manner, in any language, in whole or in part, is prohibited by the International Copyright Agreement. Under it all rights are reserved by the editor and publisher.

The editor has done his best to ensure all information appearing in this book is totally accurate. However, he cannot be held responsible by readers who are in any way inconvenienced or delayed.

The animal track illustrations have been taken from A FIELD GUIDE TO ANIMAL TRACKS, second edition by Olaus J. Murie. Copyright © 1974 by Margaret E. Murie. Reprinted by permission of the publisher, Houghlin Mifflin Company.

Typesetters: Colonial Cooperative Press, Inc., Clinton, MA 01510
Printers: Bradford & Bigelow, Danvers, MA 01923

Library of Congress Cataloging in Publication Data
Main entry under title:

South America: river trips.

   Bibliography: p.
   Includes index.
   1. South America — Description and travel — 1951-   — Guide-books. 2. Rivers — South America — Guide-books. 3. Boats and boating — South America — Guide-books. 4. Natural history — South America. I. Bradt, George. II. Bangs, Richard, 1950-
F2211.S67   918'.0438   80-69523
ISBN 0-933982-13-5 (v. 1)

COVER PHOTO: MADRE DE DIOS RIVER–PERU, PHOTO: G. BRADT

Acknowledgments

The editor would like to thank the following people and organizations contributing the time, talent and materials making this a better book.

Bill Roberson and family introduced us to the wonders of river travel in early 1980, and we can hardly wait until the next opportunity.

Thanks go to Bill Abbott and Bob Wolfson for the opportunity to see Manú again, this time more successfully. Where to next, gentlemen?

As usual in our books the Walters family must be thanked for their continuing hospitality and friendship.

We are grateful to the Concord Finishing Company for providing the cover stock for this title.

John Chipman's advice on technical matters is always needed and always freely given, for which we are thankful.

And to our editor, Carol Blackwell, many thanks for your skill and patience; sorry deadlines were so tight.

Thanks go to the Organization of American States, the Lima Times, Houghton Mifflin Co., and the South American Explorers Club for various materials generously sent and incorporated into the text.

Our deepest gratitude goes to the contributors who add unique material to this book and give it a very special flavor. We can appreciate the time and trouble you took in preparing your material and meeting the deadline. Thank you all.

Contributors

RICHARD BANGS (SOBEC President) is incredibly young to have done all the reckless river trips listed on his resume. Stay in touch, Richard, we want to receive more descriptions like the Bio-Bio for many years, so don't take any silly chances.

GEORGE BRADT is currently attending writing school; we hope to see vast improvements soon.

RUSSELL & PENNY JENNINGS are now living in western Canada having traveled all over the world for ten years. Russell is Australian, Penny is from Canada, and as they are travel agents we hope to hear more from them in the future.

JANE ROBINSON lives to travel and see new birds. She is a talented storyteller, from Texas, able to vividly recreate her travels to remote areas all over the world.

ROBIN ROBINSON seems to spend his life winging around the U.S. and South America supervising various engineering projects. Trained as a research chemist he hopes to get back to his laboratory someday.

JOSEPH ROSENBLOOM III lives in Boston and writes for various local and national publications.

NICK RYALLS, exiled and teaching English in Rio, became a good friend there. Aside from sending his account of the rio São Francisco we haven't heard much from him recently. But we do know he is back in England surrounded by stereo equipment and drowning in Wagner.

JOHN TICHENOR (President of Back Country International) has spent three years exploring the Apurímac River in Peru. We hope he will continue his explorations and telling us about them.

Preface

When we began planning this book, nine months ago, we thought of more than thirty rivers to describe in ten minutes! The next thirty rivers would have taken only twenty minutes more, and so on. That's when we realized the scope of our undertaking; there are scores of rivers to explore in South America, and on each river there are several different trips somewhere along its length. Suddenly our original idea, which seemed so simple, was swamped with dozens of possibilities. Clearly there were only two basic options: a long catalog of possible trips with superficial details about each, or a series of books detailing a few rivers in each volume.

We decided on a few rivers in a series of books.

We began this first book with no idea where the descriptions of each river would come from. But gradually the manuscripts have arrived. When deadlines dictated 'closing' the book each contribution was edited to conform to our basic format. The editor can only ask for forgiveness and understanding from the various contributors for what he did to their manuscripts.

After our closing date a manuscript arrived written by a couple from England. They've just spent nearly two years traveling South America's jungle rivers in their inflatable dinghy. Their account includes a hair-raising description of caimans attacking their rubber boat. With this manuscript the second book in the series is off to a brisk beginning. Stay tuned.

DANCING *SHIPIBO* MAIDENS

1. Rio Magdalena
2. Rio Atrato
3. Rio Frio
4. Coastal Waterway
5. Rio Napo
6. Rio Apurímac
7. Rio Amazon
8. Rio Alto Madre de Dios
9. Rio Mamoré
10. Rio São Francisco
11. Rio Bio-Bio

Contents

Acknowledgments	3
Contributors	3
Preface	4
Preparations	
Getting to South America	9
When to Go	9
Equipment	10
Photography	12
Health	12
Security	18
Maps	20
Shopping	21
Border Crossings	21
Budgeting	22
On the River	
Transportation	23
Jungle Cuisine	26
Organizing Your Own River Trip	27
Natural History	
Jungle Ecology	30
Forest Types	30
People of the Amazon Basin	32
Slash & Burn	32
Animals	33
Insects	42
Birds	43
Wildlife Viewing	47
Rivers	
North of the Amazon Basin	50
1. Magdalena (Colombia)	51
2. Atrato (Colombia)	52
3. Frio (Colombia)	54
4. Coastal Waterway (Ecuador)	56
Amazon Basin: North, West, South	58
5. Napo (Ecuador)	59
6. Apurímac (Peru)	62
7. Amazon (Peru & Brazil)	66
8. Alto Madre de Dios (Peru)	70
9. Mamoré (Bolivia)	75
South of the Amazon Basin	80
10. São Francisco (Brazil)	81
11. Bio-Bio (Chile)	85
Appendices	
U.S. & Metric Equivalents	91
Dictionary: Spanish & Portuguese	92
Museums, Zoos, Botanical Gardens	93
Service Organizations	94
Whitewater	95
Making Your Own Tropical Tent	96
Building a Balsa Raft	99
Bibliography	100
Index	103

ELABORATE FEATHER HEADDRESS

Preparations

Getting to South America

A visit to your local travel agent is all that's needed to begin your trip to South America. There are basic twenty-one day excursion fares and a variety of other plans to choose from. Because many of the ports along the rivers that are described in this book have airports it is possible to fly direct from North America or Europe to the Amazon basin. If the international airport isn't near the port you have chosen to start from, there will be a connecting flight to it. Since these short hops don't often cross international boundaries, it is best to fly direct to the country you expect to explore.

When we first began this project we thought to list all the cargo boats carrying passengers directly from Europe and North America to Belém, Manaus, and Iquitos. We have since discovered that such service no longer exists. However, it is possible to travel to many South American ocean ports by freighter and from there fly or travel overland to your river.

When to Go

Drained by the Amazon, the eastern lowlands of South America normally experience their rainy season (*invierno*) from the beginning of October to the end of April; the dry months (*verano*) extend from May through September. There are variations, but most of the average annual rainfall of 2,500 mm. falls during the winter months. However when the sun begins heating up the jungle canopy, powerful convection currents send the humid, hot air aloft. By noon you can see the clouds forming, and by two there is almost always a brief, intense storm or thunder-shower.

The best time to travel each river is listed within the fact box for that particular river, but in general, river travel is possible and comfortable from May through September.

However, during the transition months between the wet and dry seasons there may be the occasional, short-lived flooding common to the area. Even in these conditions the larger boats continue traveling, while all canoes halt until the flood recedes. At no time during the year is traveling by jungle river as easy and predictable as traveling by road. Delays must always be anticipated.

Equipment

Taking the right clothing will make your trip more comfortable. All the areas covered in this book are hot and humid except the south of Chile. Everyone has their own ideas how to dress for this climate, and may indeed already be prepared. But let us state our proven, simple formula: light-colored cotton for protection from the sun and for general comfort during the day; wool for protection from the damp coolness at night.

Artificial fibers are not cool, though they do wash and dry easily. Articles made of down, such as sleeping bags and vests, absorb moisture from the air and body. There is no way to dry down completely in the tropics so it is not particularly suitable. Wool does not absorb humidity, and even when wet it provides warmth.

As detailed in the SHOPPING section, you may wish to buy various woolens in South America, especially if you are visiting the highlands prior to your jungle trip. Otherwise, we suggest bringing these items with you, since buying wool in the jungle is not easy.

In addition to clothing you may want to consider: clothesline and pegs, towel, toilet paper, flashlight (with extra batteries), matches, candles, mug, spoon, plate, sauces and condiments, drink powders for improving the taste of purified water, ear plugs, and a spare set of contacts or glasses. Fishing gear, folding fan, umbrella, and various miniature entertainments, i.e., chess, cards, etc. Pens, pencils, writing paper, notebook, several good paperbacks for reading and swapping.

Duffel Bag

Your duffel bag is very important equipment: it is your suitcase. Duffels can be packed into a greater variety of spaces than hard suitcases. Your bag should be made of water resistant nylon, with a heavy duty zipper, shoulder strap and a zippered outside pocket. It should not be any longer than .75 m. (30″) and not more than 1 m. (40″) in circumference.

Packing your duffel takes skill which begins by keeping everything you bring to a minimum. What you bring should be neatly folded, not bunched, and placed in layers. In the bottom go the items you won't be needing often, and can be recognized by touch. Different sized plastic bags are useful for keeping groups of clothes together or dry.

All city clothes should be carried in a separate bag and left behind when you do your river trip if you are making a large circle and returning to your point of origin. If you are not, then bring even less if weight and bulk are important considerations.

In our duffel bag we keep three little bags: a ditty bag, a medicine bag and a sponge bag. All have a purpose, but basically the bags keep small, similar often-used items together. You can buy these bags or make them. Each should be a different color, size or texture for easy identification.

A ditty bag is useful for oddments such as sewing kits, fish hooks, dental floss, matches, safety pins, pens, pencils, etc.

The medicine bag should contain your malaria drug supply (better to have another cache in your main duffel), prescription drugs, aspirin, lomotil, foot-powder, dramamine, antiseptic cream, electrolyte replacement, thermometer, and something to take the itch out of insect bites such as meat tenderizer. Various emergency drugs should be kept here: penicillin, ampicillin, tetracycline, etc.

Your sponge bag contains toothbrush and paste, small mirror, razor and blades, soap, shampoo, lip salve, handcream,

Day Pack

Whether you are traveling in an open canoe or cargo boat bring a day pack (or bag) along with you. Chances are your main duffel bag will be stowed toward the bow of the canoe, or in a general cargo area. Even if you have a cabin you don't want to spend all day climbing up and down.

If you are traveling in a canoe you will need to be ready for rapidly changing conditions: breakdowns, pushing, insects, strong sun, rain squalls and wind. Cotton clothes, light in color and loose fitting, are the most comfortable daytime wear, along with sneakers, and a hat which won't blow off. In the early morning, or after a squall, the windchill factor should be anticipated by keeping both a waterproof windbreaker and a light sweater easily accessible.

You will also want to have the following items handy: water container, water purifying process, toilet paper, pocket knife, suntan lotion, soap for clothes and/or body, sunglasses, cushion, camera equipment, possibly binoculars, and small entertainments such as a paperback or writing pad. Don't forget to pack your bathing suit.

Presents

A vital part of your luggage should include presents for helpful villagers you'll meet in remote areas. We have found that postcards of your own country or family photos are the most appreciated, and least degrading and corrupting presents you can give. Cityscapes are more prized than pretty scenery.

Practical gifts should be considered and need not be costly. They should be choosen for comfort, practicality and durability. We urge you not to give things which will eventually break or wear out and cause great disappointment, such as a disposable flashlight. These items can also be swapped for things you will see along your route.

We don't hand out money or sweets because we believe that to do so eventually corrupts and debases social structures. This is, however, part of a long, complex series of bigger questions. The reason for taking presents is, quite simply, that you will receive a great deal of hospitality and you will want to reciprocate. Needles, thread, buttons, blanket pins, notebooks, ballpoint pens, pencils, barrettes, ribbons, hand-mirrors, fish hooks, fishing line, and salt make appropriate and welcome gifts. If you are nearing the end of your trip and wish to give away some of your more basic equipment, it will be received gratefully.

Photography

The basics of jungle photography are simple: a slow lens, fast film, a tripod and lots of luck. Your opportunities for photography will be more frequent, less demanding and more rewarding from your boat than from the jungle floor.

A critical problem for photographers is keeping the camera handy, ready for quick use, and protecting it from a dunking if you suddenly find yourself outside the boat. The camera should be secured by something more than just a neck or shoulder strap which could loop off in a crisis.

For cameras not in use there are double-lined, inflatable bags which not only protect your camera from hard knocks but will keep it afloat and dry should everything go overboard. A cheaper alternative is the navy surplus rubber bag used by frogmen and divers: it is thick and secured by a folded-over top with toggles.

Health

South America is not the hot bed of disease you may imagine, but certain precautions should be taken before you go, and knowing how to deal with common medical problems is useful.

And don't forget your medical insurance.

MEDICAL PROBLEMS

That we list the most common health problems and their treatment does not mean you shouldn't visit a doctor in South America. Even if the medical setup down there isn't quite what you're accustomed to, remember that doctors in Latin America are well versed in diagnosing and treating local diseases.

We realize, however, that many travelers are unable, or unwilling, to consult a doctor. In these cases pharmacists can be very helpful; they treat the local population for minor complaints. But check the expiration date on any medicines they prescribe. Many drugs, available only on prescription in the U.S.A., or Britain, are available over the counter in South America, and they're often cheaper, so don't worry about replacing your basic medical supplies there.

Remember that prevention is better than cure. Sterilize all water (even pure-looking mountain streams are often contaminated) with tincture of iodine, Halazone or Sterotab purifying tablets. Peel fruit and avoid salads and other raw vegetables.

Diarrhea Almost everyone comes down with the trots in South America. Travelers' diarrhea is caused by the bacteria *Escherischia coli* which everyone has in his intestines. The trouble is each geographical area has its own strain of *E. coli*, and these alien strains cause inflammation of the intestine and diarrhea. Nowadays the best treatment is considered to be the antibiotic oxycycline. This prescription drug can be used prophylactically if you're planning a short vacation, but should not be used over long periods.

Our method of prevention is to gradually build up a nice collection of South American *E. coli* in our intestines. It has worked beautifully and we very rarely get diarrhea nowadays. We're very careful for the first few weeks, then start to relax. We also carry Lomotil just in case.

Many people prefer to avoid taking strong medication for a simple attack of *turista*. Take plenty of fluids, and sip a solution of salt (¾ teaspoon), baking soda (½ teaspoon), potassium chloride (¼ teaspoon), and sugar or dextrose (4 teaspoons). This 'electrolyte replacement' formula is effective and safe. Make up several packets before leaving home.

Dysentery If, in addition to diarrhea, you have severe stomach cramps, pass blood in your feces, and run a fever, then you probably have dysentery. A doctor or a clinical laboratory (*analisis clínico*) should confirm the diagnosis before you take medication. Flagyl is effective for amoebic dysentery, as is tetracycline, but in a very severe case when there is also vomiting, get an injection of Dehidroemetina.

Fever If you develop a fever for any reason you should rest and take aspirin. But bring a supply of ampicillin, penicillin, or tetracycline with you since you could be struck by some infection in a hopelessly inconvenient place. Under these circumstances, take an antibiotic three times a day, but not for longer than four days without seeing a doctor.

Heat exhaustion If you over-exert yourself in very high temperatures, you are likely to be affected by the symptoms of heat exhaustion. Your body is simply telling you it can't cope much longer. Blood rushes to the skin depriving the brain and other vital organs. You will feel faint, nauseous, and have a rapid, fluttery heartbeat. Your face will be pale, and your skin, cold and clammy. The condition is not dangerous, but is a clear warning to rest in the shade, sip cool liquids, and munch a high-energy trail snack. Don't continue until you feel completely better.

Heat stroke This is possibly the result of overworked sweat glands, and is a complete breakdown of the body's cooling mechanisms. It is a very serious condition and untreated can result in brain damage or even death. The symptoms are a very high body temperature and flushed, hot and dry skin. There is no recovery when the person rests, so the treatment is to bring down the body's temperature by any means possible. If there's a river handy, that's fine, but heat stroke is more likely to hit in waterless areas. Remove the victim's clothing and sponge him with water from your canteen, then fan him vigorously. Massage his arms and legs to divert blood to his extremities. Continue these activities until his temperature is normal.

Hepatitis This is common in South America, so gamma globulin injections are recommended. There's dispute over the effectiveness of these injections, but we've never met anyone who's come down with hepatitis after the injection. However, you must keep your injections on a regular basis, which poses only a slight problem for travelers on a long trip. Pharmacists will give you a shot every 6 weeks, but make sure to buy them a new disposable needle to use with the serum. If you do come down with hepatitis, do it in Lima. A revolutionary new treatment is being developed at the *Clinica San Felipe* there. Rumor has it that you're completely cured in a few days.

Motion sickness The local people are not the only ones to suffer on the rough roads in the Andes. Dramamine or Diodoquin are effective.

Malaria When we first went to Latin America we took a malaria prophylactic just like everyone else, but now we've talked with Americans who actually live and work there, we take nothing, but carry Chloroquine with us. Here's why. Malaria is becoming increasingly uncommon in Latin America, thanks to the efforts of the Malaria Eradication Program, and what remains is becoming resistant to conventional drugs. Chloroquine, taken over a long period of time can be very harmful, and the massive dose needed to combat an attack of malaria contracted while you were taking the stuff, would be very dangerous.

So we concentrate on not being bitten by mosquitoes instead; easy enough, simply use plenty of repellent and always sleep under an adequate mosquito net. We carry Chloroquine just in case. Fortunately malarial areas are well supplied with health personnel who would advise on the correct dosage in the unlikely event of your coming down with the disease despite these precautions.

It is up to you; either do what most books tell you and take a daily or weekly tablet of a mild prophylactic such as Paludrine; or follow our example.

Sores and skin infections If the infection is serious, you will need an antibiotic, taken regularly and over a period of several days, to clear it up. A slow healing sore can be speeded on its way by applications of honey or papaya.

Athletes' foot can be a problem. Catch it before it cripples you. Tinactin in powder form is usually effective, but Hilary needed a course of antibiotics. Gentian Violet, readily available in South America, is said to be a cheap and efficient treatment.

Bring foot-powder such as Desenex or Mexana, and sprinkle it between your toes night and morning; keep your socks dry and change them frequently. If you develop a persistent and very itchy red rash on your foot, this could be a type of fungus which can only be killed by tetracycline.

Another type of fungus lives in tropical rivers and can infect the ears of bathers who like to submerge their heads. If you are one of these, use ear-plugs.

In the past two years we've noticed increasing reports of visitors returning from South America with a localized skin problem which takes different forms: pimples, hard bites, or other indications that all is not well two or three months after traveling. If you have these symptoms you may be a host to an infestation of various larvae carried by a flying insect. When this insect landed on you, its cargo of unrelated critters jumped off onto you and went to work developing a good home under your skin.

If you have cause to think you might be infected, see a physician specializing in tropical diseases and be persistent until you find one of these rare doctors.

The only word of comfort we can offer is don't let this concern put you off going abroad since these same problems happen at home too.

Yellow Fever This is again increasing in the greater Amazon basin, so make certain you are inoculated against it, and that this fact is recorded in your international vaccination certificate.

JUNGLE NASTIES

Despite your preconceived ideas of anacondas and jaguars poised for attack, there are few dangers from the animal world in the jungle. Insects, however, are another matter. They can lead to itchy days and sleepless nights. Plants can be equally unpleasant if carelessly handled. However careful you are, you will get bitten or stung. Ointment or spray containing Mepyramine Maleate and Benzocaine (Waspeze or Derma Medicone are good brands), can do a lot toward relieving the itching.

Ants (*Hormigas*) Some of the jungle varieties pack a fearsome bite and/or sting. Just watch where you stand, sit or walk.

'Bocones' These blood suckers look like tiny beetles and they attack during the day and evening. Their bite is irritating, but the effect doesn't last long. Repellent is effective.

Chiggers (*Chigoes*) In our experience, these are the nastiest of all. Chiggers are tiny mites that bore into your flesh, liquefy the tissues with a secretion, then feast on the result. They're barely visible to the naked eye, but you'll be able to see the spots, which will itch, ooze and weep for days. Again, prevention is better than cure; tuck those pants into your socks and spray with diethyl toluamide repellent.

Mosquitoes (*Zancudos*) Few people like to sleep with mosquitoes whining in their ears, and there is also malaria to worry about. A good mosquito net is a must when you consider these factors. During the day repellent and suitable clothing are enough to combat them.

The choice of repellent is up to you. 'Cutters' is a very effective brand, small and light to pack, but tedious to apply. 'Off' and other spray brands are bulkier, but you can spray them on your clothing—provided you aren't wearing artificial fabrics.

Scorpions (*Escorpions*) These chaps can do a fair amount of damage, but they become aggressive only when disturbed. Don't move stones, timber, or mess around in leaflitter unless you can see what you're doing. If you need to clear a tent site, use your boots and a knife rather than your hands. If your boots spend the night outside the tent, be sure and shake them out before putting them on in the morning.

Ticks (*Garrapata*) These are plentiful and persistent in jungle areas, and savanna grasslands. You may finish a walk with hundreds of these crawlies. If removed before they dig in and start sucking your blood they're harmless. But once they've established themselves they cause an itch lasting for several days. There are few things less conducive to a peaceful night than to feel hundreds of ticks crawling around on you.

Prevention is the best cure. Pants securely tucked into thick socks are a must, and then sprayed with a repellent containing diethyl toluamide. Now and then inspect your legs for ticks; some are so small as to be practically invisible. While still on your pants you can brush them off easily with a stick. At the end of the day, take a bath with *Neko* soap (obtainable in tick countries, and powerful enough to dislodge those on your skin) and change your clothing. Before going to bed look yourself over (or share the job with a friend) with a roll of masking tape handy. Tape is an excellent way of trapping the beasts and pulling them off you. Otherwise you have to crush them between your fingernails. Be sure to inspect those warm, clammy areas so dear to a tick's heart. Once they're established, ticks must be removed with tweezers or kerosene.

Don't worry about tick fever, you won't get it.

Wasps, Bees & Hornets   Once I inadvertently shook a branch which was the nesting site for some small blue wasps. Furious at this apparent assault, they pursued me, tangled in my hair, and I ended up with my head in the river trying to get rid of them. Not a pleasant experience, so be careful not to disturb nests in any way, don't even go near them if you see any activity.

Plants   When walking in the jungle avoid casually grasping branches or shrubs. Many sport painful spines or stinging whiskers. If you need a handhold, look carefully at it first. The most dangerous plant along the trails is the Spiny Palm. The sharp, black spines are conspicuous. If you brush against them, the spines may break off under your skin and have to be removed surgically.

Snakes   It will surprise many readers to learn that far from being snake-infested, jungles harbor relatively few of these reptiles. The reason is simple; snakes, being cold-blooded, need sunlight to raise their body temperature. And there's precious little sunlight in a tropical rain forest. But there's no denying that snakes are a danger, especially in cleared areas and for the backpacker venturing into these places, our only sound advice is don't get bitten. Most of you probably know that snakes attack only when provoked or cornered so don't give them that excuse. If you keep to the trail, watch your feet, and never put your hands where you can't see them, nothing will happen to you. You may see snakes, but they will be in a hurry to get out of your way. Wearing good boots and thick socks is extra protection.

Vampire bats   These are the only jungle mammals to be dangerous to man, and only because they are rabies carriers. Vampire bats strike at night, but so subtly that most victims don't know they've been bitten until the following morning. The bats usually go for cattle and horses, but are rather partial to human big toes if they find one available. Contrary to popular opinion, these bats don't suck blood, nor do they have hollow teeth. After lulling their victim by fanning him with their rap-

-idly beating wings, they make a slashing cut with their razor-sharp canine teeth. The blood is lapped up, and there's a plentiful supply, since their saliva contains an anticoagulant.

Security

You can be put into jail fairly easily in South America. The quickest way to jail, without passing go or collecting $200, is through drug use. Yes we know Colombia grows the best *marijuana*, and that cocaine is refined from native *coca* leaves grown all over the continent. But can you imagine what a typical South American jail cell looks like? That should give you sufficient pause. If you must use drugs, use extreme caution as well: plainclothesmen offer joints, gringo hotels are busted, and sometimes drugs are planted.

POLICE

If you do get involved with police make sure you stay cool and friendly. That isn't always easy, but getting hot and hostile won't help your case. Arguing with the police is another way of going to jail, appeasing their fragile egos is the best way to handle them. Cigarettes soften the atmosphere, and often money has a calming effect. Bribes should be used only in grave emergencies, and then very discreetly.

THEFT

The best defense against thieves is to know their methods and be continually on guard. Basically, theft falls into three categories.
1. Unguarded possessions Don't leave your luggage unless you are sure it's properly guarded or under lock and key. A chain with a combination lock is extremely useful for this purpose. Combination locks are better than padlocks because thieves haven't yet learned how to pick them. Duffel bags can often be padlocked through a zipper. Think about this aspect when you buy a bag and choose one without vulnerable pockets.
   If you carry a small bag, in addition to your duffel, never put it down, always keep it under your arm or over your shoulder.
2. Thefts from the person Handbag snatching and pickpocketing are common, but avoidable. Attach a thin chain to your change purse and secure it to your pants (trousers). You can buy a lightweight chain in South America designed for this purpose. The same method protects your penknife and handbag. It's better not to carry a handbag, and never keep your valuables in it. Not only can it be snatched; it can be picked, slit, or slashed open by clever thieves.
   If you must walk about cities with your camera, keep it hidden in a

nondescript, strongly-made bag with a good shoulder strap which you can wear across your body. Make sure it can withstand a series of strong pulls.

3. Armed robbery   Fortunately this is still very rare in South America but it can happen. The most usual weapon is a knife or *machete* held to the throat while two or three other men search the victim. There's nothing you can do in such a situation except give them what they're after. This is the way money belts are robbed, and neck pouches.

Walking around lonely or slummy areas alone can be dangerous, especially at night or in the early morning. Your money and valuables are safer in a well-locked secure hotel room or in the hotel safe box.

In any country there are high-crime and low-crime areas. All cities and tourist spots have their thieves. In other parts of the country, markets, trains, and stations are all risky places where your handbag or money-bulging pockets are particularly vulnerable. Avoid crowds if you are carrying anything of value.

Here are a few hints on protecting your valuables:

Use a neck pouch, money belt, or inside pocket for cash and passports. A neck pouch is easily made from soft material that won't irritate the skin. The strap should be strong (a thin chain is suitable as it looks like jewelry) and the right length, so the pouch hangs inconspicuously under your loose clothing. A money belt is less visible (but usually won't hold a passport). Hidden under several layers of clothing, it may not even be detected in a body search. We use a zippered bag, just big enough for passports and money, with loops and snaps which allow it to be fastened to a variety of places; under clothing, round a leg under trousers, or deep in a bag where loops have been sewn to secure it. If your passport is too bulky to carry comfortably and safely, keep handy some other form of identification, such as a driver's license.

It's always a good idea to carry two pieces of identification separately. If your passport is stolen, you can at least prove who you are to sceptical, bored officials.

WOMEN TRAVELERS

South American men, especially those in authority, such as port or ship captains or border officials, are sometimes troublesome toward foreign women traveling alone. The amount of trouble depends on your point of view and general circumstances. The vast majority of their attentions simply amount to harmless flirting, but a few men may go further. In these circumstances it is well to remember that despite the wonderfully flagrant sexual posturing throughout the continent it is basically a sexually repressive society. Latinos see foreign women, represented through imported movies and books, as sexually liberated and ready for anything. Unless you truly are, offer no encouragement whatsoever to any advances. If your aren't confident traveling alone and feel capable of handling yourself, then consider joining up with some other travelers.

LEAVING LUGGAGE

Like all travelers, we finish our trips with far more luggage than when we started. Maps accumulate, we buy handicrafts, collect books, and our bags become quite unpackable. So we've become accustomed to finding a safe place to leave our unwanted luggage. We've always found a hotel that would keep a bag for us, free. Even if they charge, it isn't much and certainly preferable to carrying it all. Bring a lockable bag for this purpose, and make sure it is put under lock and key or somewhere safe. Avoid leaving luggage in gringo hotels; unfortunately your fellow travelers are not all as honest as you are and the policy of claiming your own bag invites theft. If you must use a communal luggage dump, chain your bag to something, or at least put your passport number, name, and date on it with instructions to give it to no one else.

INSURANCE

It's well worthwhile getting luggage insurance for your trip. As you will have gathered by now, robbery is a real possibility, and the knowledge that you can get reimbursed for your precious possessions helps to allay your grief.

American Express and Thomas Cook both sell good travel insurance (you might as well get medical insurance from the same company), but read the fine print carefully before you buy it. We've had more claims turned down than accepted.

Maps

If you need a map in order to get to the port you've begun your river trip from, then the standard road map of that country will usually serve your purpose. However, it is fun to check your progress during the trip by asking the names of villages and finding them on a local map. This is especially true if you are planning to disembark for a side trip or two before continuing your river trip.

Peru has distinguished itself in mapping all of its 23 departments in scales ranging from 1:500,000 to 1:800,000. And they are fine maps: clear, easy to read and shaded to indicate altitude. They are available from the I.G.M. (*Instituto Geografico Militar*) in San Isidro, a suburb of Lima. If you wish to obtain these maps for trip planning, both offices of Bradt Enterprises stock them. The general road map of Peru, distributed by the I.G.M. and Bradt Enterprises, is good for the big picture of how the rivers relate to each other.

Colombia has an enormous map of the entire country in a scale of

1:500,000. It is a wonderful map, a little bulky, but certainly all you would ever need for river travel. The I.G.M. in Bogotá is reprinting the map, and when it is ready Bradt Enterprises will stock it.

Ecuador has only a general road map available, as far as we know.

Brazil must make maps, but we have not succeeded in obtaining even a catalog of them. If you have any luck, please send us the details.

Venezuela's various oil companies put out national road maps which are all that is available. Bradt Enterprises is able usually to keep at least a few in stock.

Bolivia has only a general road map available, which we stock.

Chile, as far as we know, has nothing available covering the Bio-Bio.

Shopping

If you take everything needed you won't have any fun shopping in South America. No, that isn't quite true, but as you pack your duffel bag remember to leave room for items purchased during your trip.

If you are visiting the mountains before going to your river, we suggest you purchase any woolen articles there. We buy a blanket, or poncho, when headed toward a river trip. Not only do these make nice presents, but we find one is just right for the cool evenings on the river.

Cotton goods are not widely available in South America; you will find most clothing made from artificial fibers inside which you may find yourself gently stewing. Mosquito netting, made of cotton, is available, usually made-up, and ready to drape over your bed.

Definitely purchase a hammock in South America. The village of Roroboya, on the Ucayali River, is well known for the fine craftmanship of their pottery and bark-cloth paintings. Bark-cloth is conveniently rolled up, while pottery, spears, arrows and bows can be tiresome as you haul them in and out of boats during your trip.

For ordinary purchases you will find Leticia, Colombia the cheapest place in the Amazon basin, with Brazilian ports being the most expensive while Peruvian ports hold a middle position.

Border Crossings

If you expect to cross from one country into another during your trip you should be prepared. Under normal circumstances, in main ports of entry, there are no problems in South America. However, in the middle of nowhere, on a remote river, any problems which do arise are frustrating and time consuming. Before leaving home try to find out the various requirements of the countries you'll be visiting.

However, when you enter a remote border post you will have to deal with reality as you find it: stubborn officials behind in their knowledge of regulations, or the same man waive requirements insisted upon elsewhere. One of the common problems is that of the onward ticket, out of the country. When entering a country by river, this requirement can be painful: there may not be a way of purchasing such a ticket, you may not have the money, or wish to invest the money you do have in a ticket. Naturally, you can always get a refund on the unused part of a ticket, but this takes time. Sometimes an M.C.O. (Miscellaneous Charges Order) impresses border officials, even a receipt in your ticket can be used cleverly. A large wad of travelers checks is always impressive along with a fairly cleancut appearance.

In any case, always carry your passport, international vaccination certificate, a dozen passport-size photographs (they come in handy at borders where they're expensive to obtain) and an alternative form of identification, such as a driver's license.

Even if no special stamp, permit, visa is needed the procedures and locations for completing border formalities are difficult to understand, even hard to find. However, it is your obligation to keep your papers in order, failure to do so could result in delays, inconvenience and possible fines. As you approach a border crossing, ask gringos you meet how they satisfied the requirements, location and hours of various offices and any special problems they encountered. Port captains, high police officials and your boat captain all may be able to shed additional light as you near the border.

Budgeting

Your travel expectations and how much time you have determine the amount of money needed for your trip. The general rule: the shorter your trip the more money needed, and *vice versa*. For an average 21 day trip a budget of $20 to $30 per day should cover all costs, including airfares. Naturally, if time isn't important you could do the same trip for $5 a day. But if you include several short air-hops you could find your budget climbing toward $50 a day.

All prices quoted in this book are approximate, and should be used as a means of comparison only. Prices listed for river trips cover the entire voyage and include all meals unless noted otherwise.

Credit cards and travelers checks can be used only in the large cities. If you plan long river trips take local currency (in small denominations) or U.S. dollars in a money belt. Large notes are not often seen in remote areas; even banks have trouble breaking them down into smaller denominations.

On the River

Transportation

The easiest, most enjoyable way to travel the Amazon basin is by river. Here and in adjacent areas to the north and south alternative means of transport do exist. Using various modes of transport adds variety to a trip, perhaps even enjoyment and efficiency. Below, the various alternatives are outlined; for more detail see *The South American Handbook*.

MOUNTAIN ROADS

There are people, those who enjoy riding roller-coasters for instance, who wouldn't mind looking out the bus window and seeing nothing except jungle 500 m. below. However, if you suffer from motion sickness or vertigo you should perhaps take a train or fly over the Andes. Mountain roads are narrow, winding, and rough. Landslides and washouts are common, especially at the start of the rains. The heaviest traffic on these roads, trucks, are taking produce and people to market. While it doesn't cost much to ride a truck with everyone else, and the view is superb, progress is slow and the climate takes a toll.

Traveling by bus is a more realistic alternative. Often you will be able to find express bus service. Collective taxis provide efficient, if somewhat crowded, service.

By traveling the mountain roads, if you have the strength, time and stamina, you will come to grips with two of the basic factors affecting all of South America: climate and mountains.

JUNGLE ROADS

Everyone knows already about the incredibly long and useful highway system Brazil has constructed through the Amazon basin. It is certainly the most extensive, ambitious and far-sighted jungle road-building project undertaken in South America; and what is more, it is virtually complete. Not only is this network of roads good, but you'll find plenty of high speed, efficient buses traversing all routes. Here, unlike the rest of South America, you'll actually be able to reserve seats; some buses have seats converting into beds for night travel.

JUNGLE RAILROADS

There are not many railroads in the jungles of South America because the rivers have always been a cheaper alternative to the enormous capital outlay involved in building a railway. One notable exception is the route starting in São Paulo, or Rio de Janeiro, and ending in La Paz. It isn't an easy trip, or fast, but it is most interesting.

Most of the railroads in the jungle start in the highlands. These afford an alternative to the bumpy, torturous vehicular roads which may not appeal to those suffering from vertigo or motion sickness. And these trains provide a wonderful opportunity to observe vegetation changes at close range.

Here is a list of the trains connecting various ports mentioned in this book. Schedules should be verified, and seats reserved, as soon as possible if you are certain a particular train trip is in your future. We suggest paying a little more and going first or second class.

Brazil   São Paulo (or Rio de Janeiro) to La Paz, Bolivia via Campo Grande, Santa Cruz, Cochabamba La Paz. Short bus trip from Santa Cruz takes you to Puerto Villaroel and the Rio Mamoré.

Salvador—Juazeiro, connects with the Rio São Francisco Puerto Vêlho—Guajará Mirim, connects with the Rio Mamoré (Bolivia) and the Rio Madiera (Brazil).

Colombia   Bogotá to Barranquilla or Santa Marta via Puerto Berrío Rio Magdalena. This railroad is responsible for the fading river traffic on the Magdalena.

Ecuador   Quito—Esmeraldas connects with the Coastal Waterway on the southern end.

San Lorenzo—Ibarra connects this with the highlands on the northern end of the waterway route.

JUNGLE AIRPLANES

Rarely is it necessary to stay on a boat for more than five days before you arrive at a port with air connections to other parts of the jungle or to the capital of the area. And, if you are really short of time, you can see the jungle, rivers and villages by plane: TANS (*Transportes Aéreos Nacionales de la Selva*) runs a float plane between Pucallpa and Iquitos three times a week, returning on the alternate days. The trip takes all day, with frequent stops, and would be an interesting introduction to the area.

But you should remember a few things if you intend to do any flying around the Amazon:

1. Make reservations as soon as possible upon arriving in the country, and confirm them as often as you can. If you're traveling on a remote river and unable to do your own confirming, have a friend keep confirming your reservations for you.

2. Upon arriving in the town you plan to fly out of, visit the airline office or airport for the latest news. Sometimes due to equipment failure or bad weather, there is a large crowd waiting to get on the same plane. Under these circumstances don't be afraid to be pushy; find the headman and talk to him, explaining your situation.

3. If you are stranded you will need all your powers of imagination, persistence and Spanish. Start asking around for alternative flights back to civilization. They may not take you to exactly where you want to go, but you'll get somewhere! The army has bases throughout all countries in South America and often these bases are supplied by air. We've traveled on army cargo planes; they aren't comfortable, but at least you're moving.

RIVER TRANSPORT

If you are traveling by raft, canoe or motorized canoe you will have to stop for the night and camp. The narrow rivers are too dangerous for small craft to navigate at night. If you are traveling in this style you will obviously need the basics for camping: cooking and eating equipment, as well as sleeping gear.

We recommend this mode as the best way to see the rivers in the upper Amazon basin. At all times you will be in close contact with what you've come to see: nature. As Jane Robinson explains, not only can you see more from the river but it is so much more comfortable than slogging through the jungle. Sitting beside a blazing fire of driftwood, with good friends and a bottle of rum, on a remote sandbank, is our idea of real fun. It's a tropical version of Huck Finn, and look at the fun he had!

The next step up is to travel by cargo boat, which also carries a few passengers. The rivers these boats traverse are not deep or wide enough to allow a night passage. These boats are tied up to the riverbank at night, and the passengers sleep on board, in hammocks. Since cargo takes precedence over passengers it isn't always easy finding a place to sling your hammock. If there are no hooks to hang your hammock from, there are always beams and supports. There will always be enough room to sling your hammock under some cover out of the rain. Don't forget to use your mosquito netting.

On the Mamoré (Bolivia) we slept inside our mosquito netting tent 'pitched' on the tiny deck behind the wheelhouse, the only patch of deck large enough for our 2 m. $\times$ 2 m. tent.

Sanitation facilities do exist, but they're primitive. In a curtained area in the stern of the boat you'll usually find a toilet and shower. You will soon get used to this strange arrangement throughout the tropics.

Meals are often eaten in your hammock, or while standing around near the kitchen. Not only are the meals quick, they are boring: rice and beans with a sliver of nondescript meat and a bit of sauce for color. With slight variation this is it, folks, three meals a day. The monotony is sometimes broken by fried, crispy bananas.

Thus you might want to think about bringing on board some sort of supplemental food, fruit or a tasty condiment to add variety and zip. At mealtimes you may see a large jar of pickled carrots, onions and chilies. Talk about zip: a tiny piece of carrot could burn your mouth for hours. If the vegetables are too *picante,* try a little of the liquid, cautiously. Having sampled one jar and found it not to your taste doesn't mean the next one won't be—keep trying. It has to do with how long the mixture has been steeping together.

The next step up takes you, literally, as high above the water as you are likely to get; onto some sort of craft with cabins. This is where the class system begins; deck, hammock and cabin. In cabin class, apparently, there is a breeze, along with an improved view of the jungle's vastness and greater varieties of pasta are served.

JUNGLE CUISINE

Eating and drinking strange and mysterious items is lots of fun, so long as it isn't carried too far. This is not a complete list of exotic jungle fare, you will find other foods mentioned in the text, but an attempt at covering the high points. Naturally we wouldn't want to take the fun out of it all by listing everything; don't be afraid to experiment.

Juices	Sucos	Jugos
Pineapple	*Abacaxi*	*Piña*
Breadfruit	*Fruta do Conde*	*Chirimoya*
Guava	*Goiaba*	*Goyaba*
Passion Fruit	*Maracuja*	*Maracuya*
Tamarind	*Tamarindo*	*Tamarindo*

Main Dishes

Cooked Salted Banana	*Tachacho*
Fried Salt Pork	*Cecina*
Mashed Yucca, boiled	*Jaune de Yuca*
Boiled Banana	*Inguiri*
Barbecued Fish	*Pataraschca*
Raw Fish, 'Cooked' in Lemon	*Cebiche* (Peru's national dish)
Black Beans & Various Meats, Herbs	*Feijoda* (Brazil's national dish)

Dessert

Fried Cassava Flour & Molasses	*Picarones*

Organizing Your Own River Trip

It's one thing to get on a cargo boat, sling your hammock and get off when you reach your destination. It's something else again to organize your own river trip. It can be done, and done well, with a minimum of fuss and hassle. It takes a spirit of adventure, and someone who is a practical, farsighted organizer. What follows is a random and incomplete collection of thoughts from the little experience we've had on river trips.

Before going any further we must stress that even the best organized trips run into delays. They're unavoidable. For every three days you expect to travel, add another day for miscellaneous delays. Better to get back a few days early with a little food left over than miss your plane connections and starve.

Take everything you'll need with you. Don't expect to buy it along the way; it may not be in season, available or heard of. Bring a drum of gasoline, if practical. And plenty of cash. Someone in the group should have a good, basic command of Spanish; nothing fancy, just the basics.

When you find a canoe for hire keep your negotiations amicable, practical and basic. For instance, make certain the owner (*el dueno*) knows where you want to go, how long you expect to stay and when you have to be back. As things progress make notes; now and then repeat questions in a different way just to make sure you understand what is being said.

It is customary on river trips for the visitors to feed (though not house) the crew. There will always be a minimum of two crew: the owner and his assistant. So plan your provisions accordingly.

Canoes always leak, so make sure the bottom layer of your luggage pile is waterproof, or resting on floorboards. And bring plastic for a luggage cover. Consider what passengers will sit on. There must be enough space between the seats for knees, the things that stick out when a person sits down; putting too many people in too small a boat will result in knee-eating 8, 10 or 12 hours daily.

Extra weight is a double problem: your canoe will sink lower into the water slowing your progress, and you'll need more water in the river. Inevitably you will get fewer kilometers to a liter of precious gasoline.

To go as far as possible all duffels must be cut to a minimum of bulk and weight. Ideally, one person's duff, sleeping gear included, should fit into one bag no longer than .75 m. and no more than 1 m. in circumference. Nobody should need more than 20 kg. of baggage on a river trip. Essentials must be put into small plastic bags, within duffels, in case everything goes into the water. Plastic garbage bags can be used to cover sleeping bags if not inside duffels. However, lots of small bags in a canoe make carrying, packing and salvage operations time consuming so all efforts should be made to cram little bags into big ones, or at least tied together.

A full 55 gallon (208 liter) drum of gasoline weighs about 150 kg., or the equivalent of a passenger with luggage. Depending on many variables you might need to carry two full drums; consider this when planning your trip.

A drum of gasoline always contains about a gallon of high octane water, which fortunately sinks to the bottom. By tilting the drum as you siphon the gas, all the water will collect in the very bottom of the tilt. When you have siphoned off about 200 liters, carefully keeping the hose off the bottom of the drum, start siphoning the last 8 liters into a shallow bowl. You'll see the water; it's gray and collects in the bottom of the bowl. Decant the gas, throw away the water.

The hardest part of the gasoline operation is starting the siphon without getting a mouthful of gasoline. The locals don't seem to mind, but most gringos do. If you can lower the hose (*manga*) until it is full of gas, then cover the end you are holding. Pull the hose out and put the end you're covering into another drum, but make sure the hose outside is lower than the end of the hose inside. Then uncover your end. You should be rewarded by a gurgle and a fine rush of gas.

Organizing an independent, successful river trip from scratch is a rewarding experience. During the trip there will be problems and frustrations, but you'll look back on the trip as an adventure.

LEADING QUESTIONS

Out of their eagerness to help, many South Americans try to anticipate the response to questions from gringos. The question: "Does this boat leave tomorrow?" will invariably be answered by, "Yes." Any question asked in this way will get a similar answer.

A more sensible question would be: "Do you know when this boat leaves?" This requires positive thinking. If the answer is yes, then you might ask when this is likely to happen. If you get an estimate, by all means check it out with other people in the area, but always start from the same question. Once you have asked five or six people you can start evaluating the answers. Until you get at least three people agreeing on something, don't put much faith in the answer.

If you intend visiting a national park on your own make certain you have all the required papers with you. The more remote parks are almost certain to require a permit of visitors. Others frequented by tourists don't often require permits, and if they do your group leader will get one. But by all means find out. It would be terrible to travel for two or three days, perhaps longer, and be turned back because you didn't have a piece of paper. Don't forget to allow enough time to secure the permit.

Natural History

COLLARED TROGON

Near the equator, South America's steamy jungles produce mysterious fruits. On a canoe trip down a narrow backwater our guide brought us two edible mysteries. One, nearly the size of a basketball, was covered with a stubble of thorns on a woody shell. With a machete he cut off the thorns, gashed the wood and drank. Following his example we found a slightly acidic, refreshing milk. After draining one segment, the ball was turned and gashed again, exposing another well of liquid. The whole thing resembled a compartmentalized coconut.

The next day our guide gave us a second mysterious fruit, showing us how to peel it and remove the seeds. After a cautious exploratory taste we ate greedily. The pulp was exquisitely fragrant, and delicious. After finishing, we clamored for more.

"No. One is enough. Now you must wait."

"Wait?" Wait for what, we wondered.

Then we realized the juicy pulp had changed. It now hung about our hands and mouths like chewing gum. My beard was a total write off. Pulling didn't help, nor did scraping. Our guide began laughing, and we would have joined him, but it isn't easy laughing with your lips glued together. As his laughter continued we began to feel a bit frantic. After making hysterical gestures our guide produced a bottle of whisky. A blessed solvent. In no time we were cleaned up and could join the mirth.

Jungle Ecology

The rain forests visible today haven't changed much in sixty million years. During that time, of course, a succession of flora and fauna have evolved, flourished and died only to be replaced by others better adapted to the changing conditions.

Almost all the flora and fauna of the tropical forests live within the tree canopy. The trees provide both haven and food to a myriad of interrelated life-forms.

Here trees have adapted differing strategies for growth and propagation, as have the life-forms they host. Their crown of leaves, for instance, is shaped differently depending on their height in order to catch the maximum available sunlight. Their all important blossoms and seeds (fruits) must be available at just the right time, in just the right way, in order to reach just the right place for the best chances of germination and growth.

Certain trees have developed a strategy of blossoming and fruiting four times annually, while others conserve their energy for a long burst of blossoms once every two years. Obviously, if all the blossoms came out at once there wouldn't be enough pollinaters to fertilize the waiting blossoms. Nor would there be enough fruit-eaters available to eat all the fruit and distribute the seeds. Many of the seeds are eaten by insects, but the most successful of all jungle trees (*Leguminosae*) has developed an insect-proof seed pod, temporarily at least.

The *anopheles* mosquito was happily, harmlessly living in the jungle canopy until its habitat began being destroyed. As the forests were felled the *anopheles* found herself on our level and quickly realized human beings could be successfully injected with larvae. In the years since we find different strains of malaria cropping up around the world. One very rare type, cerebral malaria, is successful in decimating remote populations because it is on a fifty year life cycle, or two generations. By the time the fifty years are up the survivors can no longer remember the event, nor can researchers immediately realize the type and treat it specially.

Forest Types

South America is the only continent on which all five distinct jungle forest types are found. In your travels you may be able to notice the transition between forest types, but usually the change is affected more subtly, depending on elevation, prevailing winds and temperatures. Unfortunately, there is no one place where all five forests can be seen in neat succession. In our survey we well start at the top of the Andes, plunge to the lowest, hottest and most dense jungle forest on the equator, then work our way north and south.

CLOUD FOREST

As you drive up the dry, western slopes of the Andes, cross their spine, and start down you will inevitably hit fog. Humid, warm air from the Amazon basin is forced up by prevailing winds blowing toward the Pacific. As the air rises it cools, wringing the moisture out of it. The twisted, gnarled, dwarf-trees are shaped by the wind. They support various airplants, nurtured by the relatively warm air and fog. The plants and grasses surrounding the trees are also there, and specially adapted, because of the climate; they flourish inspite of little sun and withstand constant fog and wind. It's a unique ecological niche populated by familiar species successfully adapted to this unusually severe environment.

ECUATORIAL RAIN FOREST

This is what most people think of as The Jungle. It covers the entire Amazon basin, limited only by altitude and latitude. Conditions throughout the basin are remarkably stable: rainfall between 2,500–3,000 mm. annually, an average annual temperature of 27°C. and a tree canopy at a height of 30–40 meters. Most of the life in this area is in the tree tops for nutrients and sunlight.

SUBTROPICAL FOREST

This forest is usually encountered directly north or south of the Amazon basin. Conditions here vary more than in the Amazon: temperatures range from 15°C.–25°C. and rainfall amounts to about 1,000 mm. annually. There are noticeable wet and dry seasons. The Rio São Francisco, and Rio Mamoré, flow through this type of forest.

MONSOON RAIN FOREST

This type of forest is found in only two areas of South America: Colombia and Brazil. Moisture laden winds being forced up a high land mass near an ocean between 5°–10° north or south of the equator account for the heavy annual rainfall: 8,992 mm. (354") in Quibdó, Colombia. Temperatures here fluctuate between 20°C.–25°C. The Rio Atrato flows through a monsoon rain forest.

TEMPERATE RAIN FOREST

Still further from the equator, and thus colder, the temperate rain forests grow in many of the first and second world countries. The eastern reaches of the Rio Bio-Bio flow through this type of forest in southern Chile.

The People of the Amazon Basin

The vast majority of people you will see on your trip anywhere within the Amazon basin are simple, country peasants no matter whether they're Indians, whites, blacks or some mixture. Outside the several commercial centers, you will find most people living off the land. The land in the basin is poor, lacking in essential nutrients, but with a stable climate. Without a great deal of work, or high level technology, these peasants have learned to live from what the land provides. And the land doesn't provide much; but what is harvested is cleverly adapted to keep the population alive.

Skills learned, practiced and refined over the centuries enable the people to live by what they get. All they have by way of knowledge, experience and wealth is the land and their relationship with it. If people in the area seek more, they must go elsewhere. Advancement up the ladder to success isn't possible here because there is no ladder.

Because the jungle will provide, and there is only what the jungle provides, most of the time here is spent waiting. There isn't much else to do, and very little else is possible. There exists a heavy sense of sameness, of inevitability. The few things that must be done are simple tasks, easily mastered by an unschooled people and shared among extended family members.

All this is difficult to understand from within our own sensibilities shaped by the internal combustion engine, temperate climates and incredibly fertile lands everywhere we look. Coming to grips with opposing realities is one of the best reasons for traveling the Amazon basin.

Slash and Burn

As you travel throughout the jungles and forests of South America you will see areas in various stages of destruction. These areas are being cleared of all vegetation for a unique type of subsistence farming. This controversial practice has wide implications for the planet, so we decided a little research was in order; the results are surprising.

Popular belief holds that the world's jungles are standing on rich, fertile land. This belief is wrong: the soil supporting jungle forests is poor in nutrients because heavy rains wash any nutrients from decaying leaf-litter right down through the porous soil out of reach of any vegetation.

Slashing and burning has been practiced within all the vegetation belts for the last seven thousand years, both in the northern and southern temperate forests as well as those lying along the equator. Our ancestors were slashers and burners.

With a few variations, the cycle has always been the same everywhere.

The cycle goes like this: a family builds a permanent house in a sparsely populated section of the jungle. From this central base the family ranges out to those areas selected for growing crops. Once a suitable location is found, usually it is flat and densely forested, workers begin cutting down all vegetation within a certain area, usually about 100 m. wide. Often the cutting starts toward the end of the rains so that when the sun appears all burnable material is dried by it. At the end of the dry season workers set fire to the clearing. After burning the undergrowth, smaller branches and bark, the workers move in with seeds. Depending on the type of seed they are either broadcast or planted individually in the ashes. With luck the rains arrive converting the solid ashes into liquid nutrients the growing plants can use. The farmers can usually get two years of crops before all the ash has been washed down through the soil. The family then finds another site and starts the process again. Ideally the first site should lie fallow for eighteen years. In this way only about 10% of the land is under cultivation at any one time, and supports about 65 people per square kilometer.

If the cycle is properly ordered, slashing and burning actually improves soil fertility without risk to the land itself or surrounding areas. After the farmers leave, continuing decomposition provides food for insects and maintains a fairly high nutrient level in the soil. These nutrients now provide growth for the succession of bushes and trees which will take over the clearing once more.

But population pressures, better medicines, improved transportation and modern tools have about halved the fallow periods so the slash and burn process becomes counterproductive. If an area is farmed for longer than three years the nutrients are exhausted and the forest will never regenerate. The clearing becomes grassland, a tangle of roots impossible to cultivate with primitive tools.

Currently the world is watching carefully Mr. Ludwig's papermill project in the Amazon basin. This huge experiment is basically slash and burn, but on an enormous scale with enough land for strict enforcement of the growing and fallow cycles. Nobody yet knows whether it is a commercially viable idea. It is, however, only a matter of time before population pressures and improved technology make Ludwig's dream practical for all the vast tropical forests remaining, and there aren't many left. There is still time to set aside specified forests for the continued growth of the many species of unique flora and fauna so future generations can study and enjoy them.

Animals

Red Howler monkey *Alouatta seniculus* (Spanish: *Aullador*).
Unlike most other travelers we saw howlers before we heard them. We were chugging up the Rio Atrato in our banana boat when an astonishing sight met our eyes. A tree covered in large yellow blossoms stood near the bank, its boughs festooned with enormous monkeys with rich chestnut colored bodies and black limbs. Some were nibbling

the blossoms, but most were hanging motionless, like huge toys. We asked our captain what they were. *"Aullador,"* he replied, and illustrated his answer by making an Indian war-cry; a passable imitation of the howl we were to hear later that day. If you camp in tropical forests you are very likely to hear this unearthly cry, even if you don't see the creatures. The sound carries for miles; from a distance it can be mistaken for the wind in the trees, but close to, it defies description. If you're not pre-warned you may think the forest is haunted.

Howler monkeys move around in troops, and the troop leader is responsible for the dawn and dusk howling concerts, although others join in. The male has a huge voice box, strengthened with cartilage, which enables him to project the sound so impressively. Being the largest of the American monkeys also helps.

Spider monkey *Ateles belzebuth (mono araña).*

They have no thumbs. Their bodies are beautifully adapted to tree life, where they are the most efficient climbers and swingers of all the New World monkeys. It's a joy to watch them moving effortlessly through the trees, making prodigious leaps, and using their tails as hands. In fact the tail has a hairless area on the underside which can feel as efficiently as a finger, so the tail really is a fifth limb.

Spider monkeys come in a great variety of colors: black, chestnut, and light brown. But you will always be able to recognize them by their long limbs.

YOUNG SPIDER MONKEY

Black-capped capuchin *Cebus apella (capuchin/negro).*

You may well have seen this monkey before you begin your trip since they make popular pets, and are the traditional organ-grinders' monkeys. They are said to be exceptionally intelligent. A troop soon made our acquaintance in the Katios park, lining up on a bough to observe us carefully. They are more inquisitive than other monkeys so you can watch them at close quarters. With their pink faces and white 'cowl' they are unmistakable, and are common in protected areas.

Coati or **coatimundi** *(gato solo, pizote).*

You are unlikely to travel far in Amazon America without meeting a coati, either in the wild or as a pet. They are playful and affectionate pets, but their long whiffly noses get into everything; they are very destructive. Coatis belong to the same family as raccoons, and live in tropical forests where they are more active in the early morning and evening, foraging in troops of up to thirty, although they may also be solitary. (I have heard that the name coatimundi refers to these solitary animals.) They are excellent tree climbers and may at first glance be mistaken for a monkey as they shinny up a tree in search of fruit or a tasty insect.

Agouti *(sereque).*

Agoutis have the misfortune to taste good, so you are unlikely to see one except in well protected parks. Indeed, relentless hunting has turned this diurnal rodent into a mainly nocturnal one in populated areas.

AGOUTI & COATI

Agouti tracks

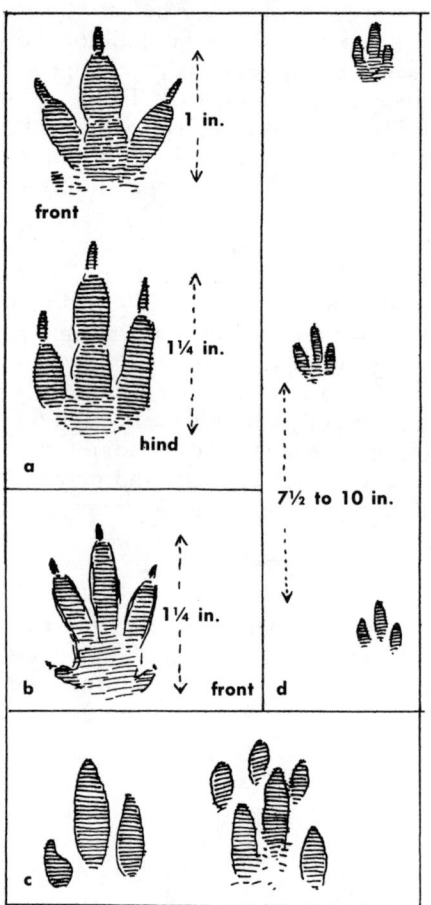

a, b, c. Tracks in mud (Panama Canal Zone, 1952).
C shows the fragmentary toe marks that one often finds.
d. Walking pattern.

Coati tracks

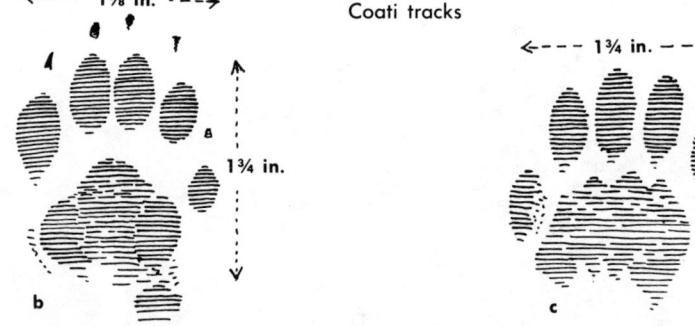

Paca *(Conejo pintado, gua-gua).*

Closely related to the agouti, but larger and with chains of white spots running down its sides, pacas are hunted enthusiastically wherever they occur. We went on a paca hunt in Colombia, and the meat was the most delicious either of us had ever tasted. Not surprisingly, this persecution has made the paca very shy and you are unlikely to see one where hunting is permitted. They occur in tropical rain forests and evergreen forests, eating fruit and seeds.

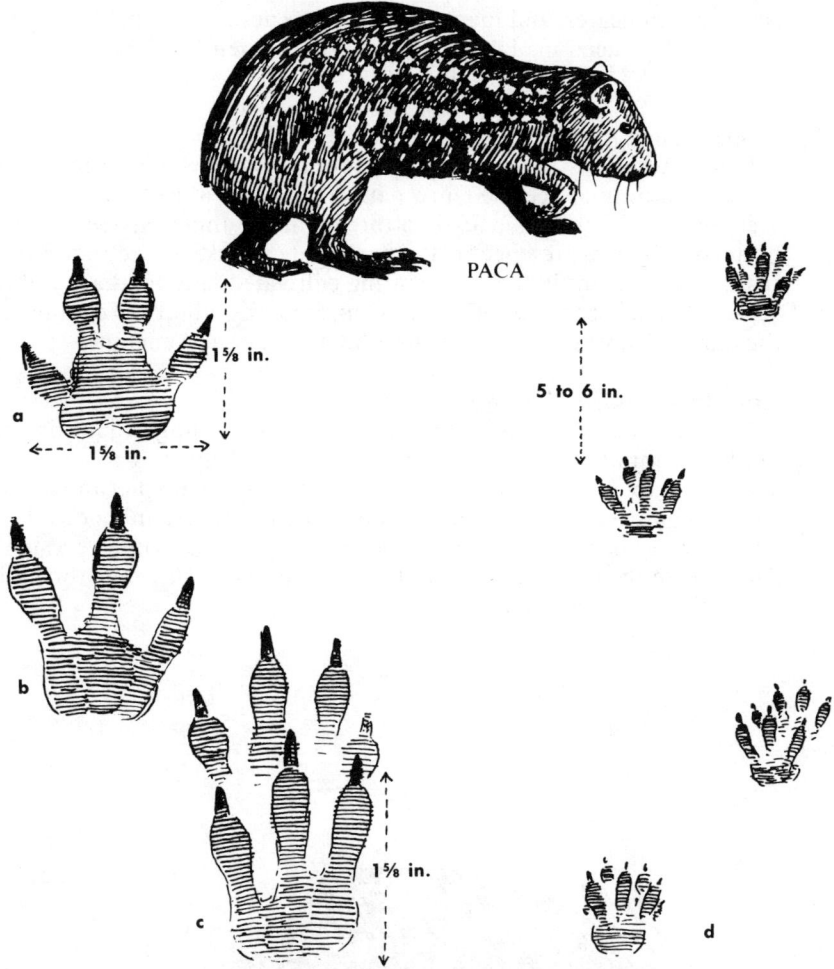

Paca sign, about ⅔ natural size, the tracks in soft mud (Canal Zone, Sept. 12, 1952)

a and b. Front and hind track, respectively.
c. Hind track partly covering front.
d. Track pattern.

Kinkajou *(mico de noche, micoleon, oso mielero).*

Having promised to include only animals that are easily seen, I cannot resist the kinkajou, although we've never seen one in the wild. My justification is that they are frequently kept as pets in Indian villages (and by gringos) and if you meet one you will have to have a heart of stone not to be completely captivated.

Kinkajous are, in fact, common in many South American rain forests, but since they are completely nocturnal and spend the day hiding away in hollow trees, you will only see one if you search at night with a flashlight. These animals are very fond of honey, as one of their Spanish names indicates, and manage to rob bees nests, despite their apparent lack of protection. They have very soft golden fur, huge eyes, low set ears, and a prehensile tail.

Striped skunk *(zorillo).*

I was on my way to the river one night to collect water when one of these little animals crossed my path a few feet ahead. Apart from arching his tail over his back in a threatening manner, he seemed unperturbed by my presence or the flashlight. Skunks are common in a variety of different habitats, including cultivated land, and are full of self-confidence because of their scent spraying ability. Fortunately they are usually content to simply threaten potential enemies.

Armadillo *(cusuco, armado).*

Certain areas seem to be full of armadillos, rustling around in the dry leaves foraging for insects. Armadillos live in burrows, so need soft soil. You may find one lapping at your water supply if you camp some way from a stream in the arid regions. Armadillos certainly need their protective armor; they have poor hearing and even poorer eyesight. Their sense of smell is excellent, however, so try to stay down-wind if you want to watch them.

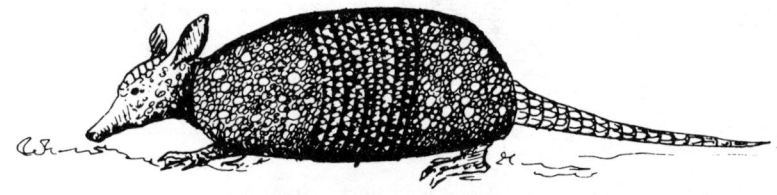

NINE-BANDED ARMADILLO

Collared peccary *(chancho de monte, zaina, javelina).*

Remember that wild adults can be dangerous animals capable of inflicting a serious wound with their sharp tusks. Peccaries live in a great variety of habitats, and being gregarious, are usually found in groups. Often you will smell a peccary before seeing it since they secrete musk from a gland in the middle of their back.

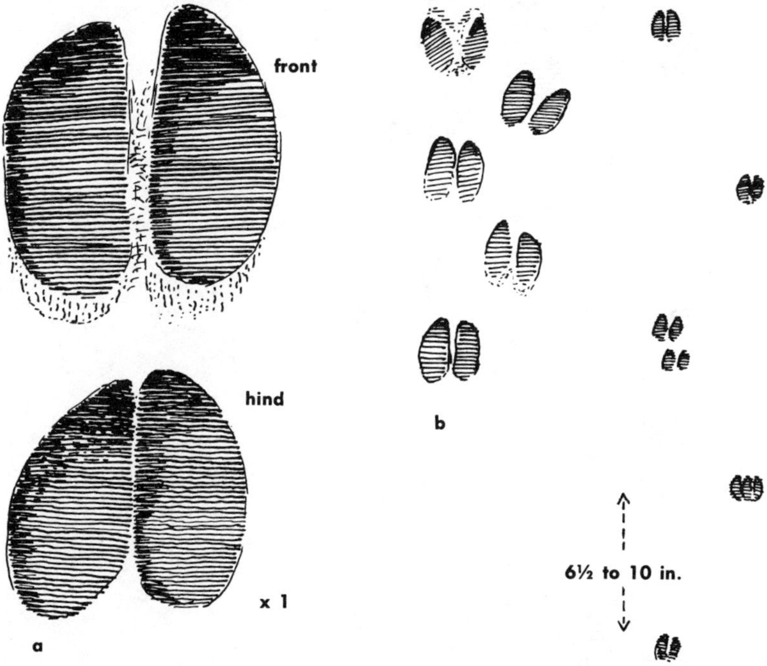

Peccary tracks

a. Typical tracks in clay, natural size. Front hoofs about 1½ in. long; hind, 1¼ in. (Fleishhacker Zoo, San Francisco).
b. Tracks in mud, showing variations (Tex. and Ariz.).
c. Track pattern, in mud. Width, or straddle, about 4 to 5 in.

Tapir *(danta)*.

An animal you probably won't see unless you're very lucky. These are large creatures, related to the horse, and weighing around 300 kg. They live in dense forest, coming out at night to feed, and are excellent swimmers. Their chief enemy is the jaguar and man.

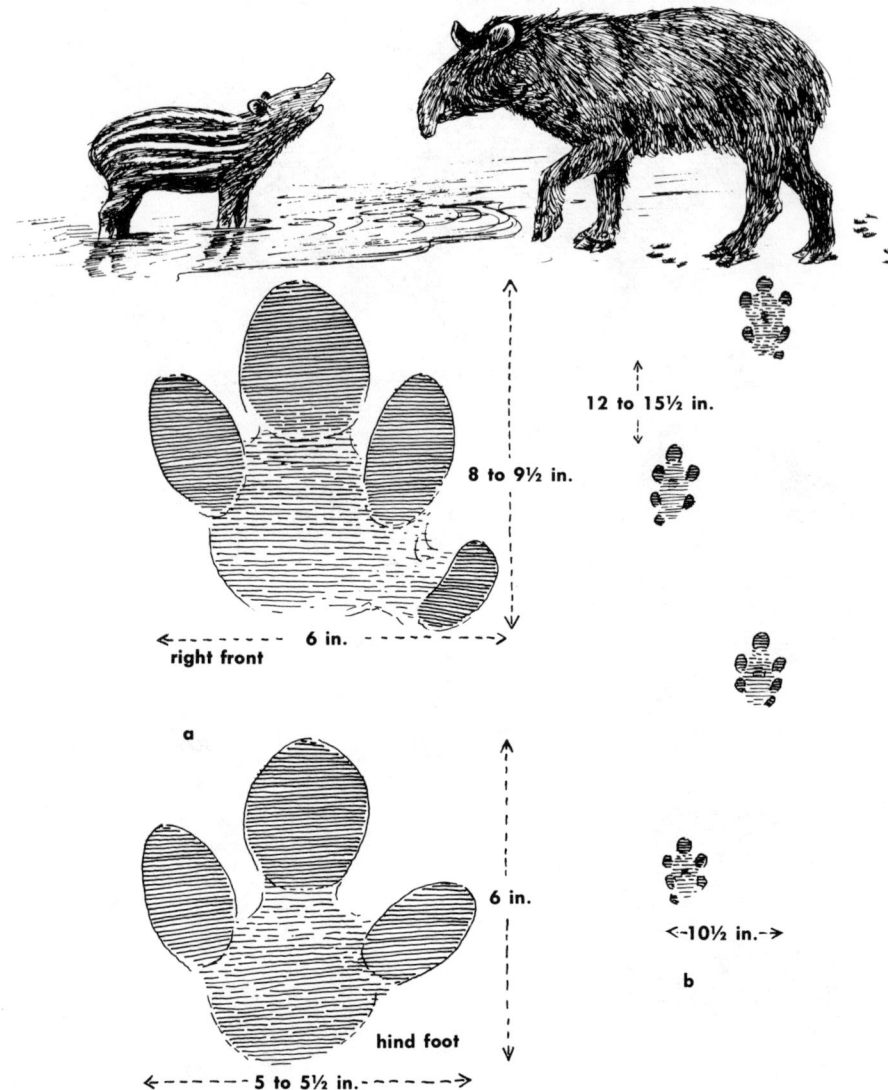

Tracks of Baird's tapir in mud

  a. Front and hind tracks.
  b. Walking trail pattern. The hind foot appears to slightly overstep the front track.

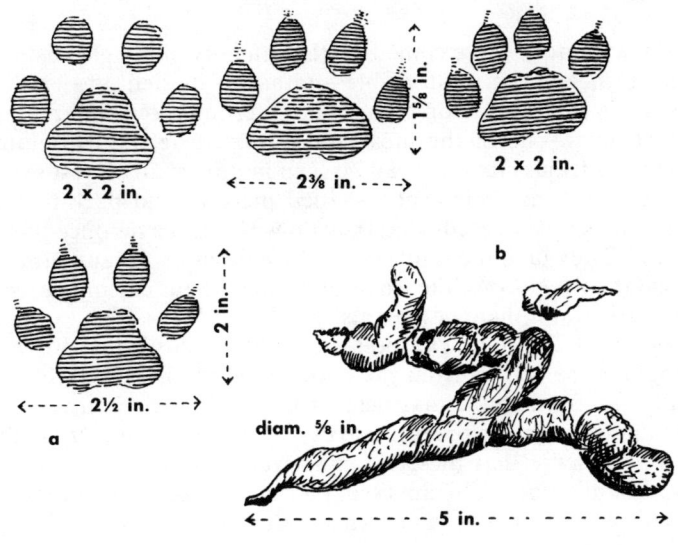

Ocelot tracks and scat
a. Tracks in sand
b. Dropping.

Jaguar tracks and scat
a. Tracks.   b. Dropping.

Insects

Although many of these come into the category of 'jungle nasties,' they are nevertheless the most visible and easily studied of all wild creatures. Let's concentrate on ants. There are numerous different species in the tropics, one of the most interesting being the **leaf-cutter ant**. These industrious creatures can be seen in almost any forest in tropical America, carrying their neatly shaped piece of leaf back to the nest. Have you ever wondered what they do with the leaves once they reach the nest? They take them to a carefully cultivated fungus garden. The ants eat the fungus (not the leaves) and the fungus can only exist in the moist dark atmosphere of the ants' 'garden.' It's a perfect example of a symbiotic relationship. The preferred tree or shrub that the ants are cutting may be 100 m. from the entrance to the nest, and this may be equally far from the actual nest. About half their journey, then, is made underground so that the leaves do not become too dry in the sun. You will observe that these foraging trails are up to 1 m. wide and cleared of all debris. The ants seem to know exactly where they're going. This is because they lay down an odor. If you look closely, you will see the ants constantly touching the ground with their antennae, smelling their way home. This chemical also probably kills off the vegetation on the trail helping to create that well-swept look.

Another interesting ant, though far less pleasant, is the **army ant**. Whereas the gentle leaf-cutter has modified its sting to produce the odor, the army ants can both bite and sting. They move through the forests in huge columns devouring everything in their way. They are capable of overwhelming and killing large insects, and are a popular source of horror in those "Jungle Tales." A human, of course, can easily get out of their way. Among the army ants are **soldier ants,** with huge heads and jaws. The Indians once used these ants to suture wounds. They would hold the ant over the wound and squeeze it so that the jaws closed holding the edges together. Then they would simply pinch off the body.

Maybe it would still work in an emergency!

Dry tropical forests are full of **arcacias** with pairs of wicked looking thorns. We found these made useful fingernail cleaners and were annoyed by the fact that there was usually a furious stinging ant concealed within the thorn. Later we learned that this is another beautiful example of a symbiotic relationship; the ants live in the hollow base of the thorns and feed on nectar produced by the leaf stems and tips. In return for this hospitality they protect the arcacia from invasion by other plants, biting off an alien shoot as soon as it enters their tree's territory.

> *Never disturb rocks or logs as creatures can jump out at you. If you wish to clear a spot in the jungle always use sticks, not hands.*

Birds

South America has approximately three thousand bird species, a third live nowhere else. No matter if you've never paid any attention to birds before, you are sure to see many strange and interesting ones you will want to identify and know a bit about. The species discussed below are the most common you will see. For more enjoyment, however, you may want to bring a pair of binoculars, a detailed guide to the birds and your life-list. In the bibliography there are two excellent guides for birdlife.

Birds active along the rivers you may already know: kingfishers, woodpeckers, blue jays, cardinals, for instance. No, these aren't the same species you know at home, but relatives filling the same ecological niches. But the real attraction of tropical rivers is the myriad of exotic birds easily visible.

The **Horned Screamer** (*Anhima cornuta*) is usually seen meandering along the water's edge. It is the size of a turkey, with disproportionately long, thick legs. They often fly to great heights and slowly circle almost out of sight. For a bird that earned a name and reputation for legendary concerts, the Horned Screamers can be remarkably silent.

As you would expect, the Amazon basin is full of parrots, but don't expect to identify many of them. You will seldom see a sitting parrot at close range and in flight they are usually too fast for their colors to distinguish them.

Macaws are the most spectacular parrot and the easiest to identify. The largest ones, 75-100 cm., are common flying over the river in pairs in the dusk, or you may see flocks of fifty or more.

The **Blue and Yellow Macaw** (*Ara ararauna*) is exceptionally beautiful and unmistakable in good light. Its upperparts, wings, and long pointed tail are blue, its underneath is yellow. The other two large macaws, **Scarlet** (*Ara macao*), **Red and Green** (*Ara chloroptera*), are separated by the small patch of color at the bend on the upperside of the wings. In the Scarlet this patch is yellow, in the Red and Green it is green.

Identifying the other 97 species of parrots living in the Amazon basin is frustrating, it's best just to enjoy their raucous chatter and flash of color as they fly.

You may not see many, but look for an occasional pair of **Moscovy Ducks** (*Cairina moschata*), the wild version of the familiar domesticated barnyard duck. Their natural habitat is not the barnyard but the edges of tropical forest streams and ponds throughout South America. These large blackish-green ducks with a large white patch on each wing are stately and attractive despite their red, warty faces.

The **Orinoco Goose** (*Meochen jubatus*) is more frequently seen standing conspicuously tall on sandbars along rivers. With its all white head and neck, reddish belly and back, it is unmistakable.

The long, hanging nests seen along rivers belong to one of several species of Amazon orioles: *oropendolas* or *caciques*. Sometimes they're

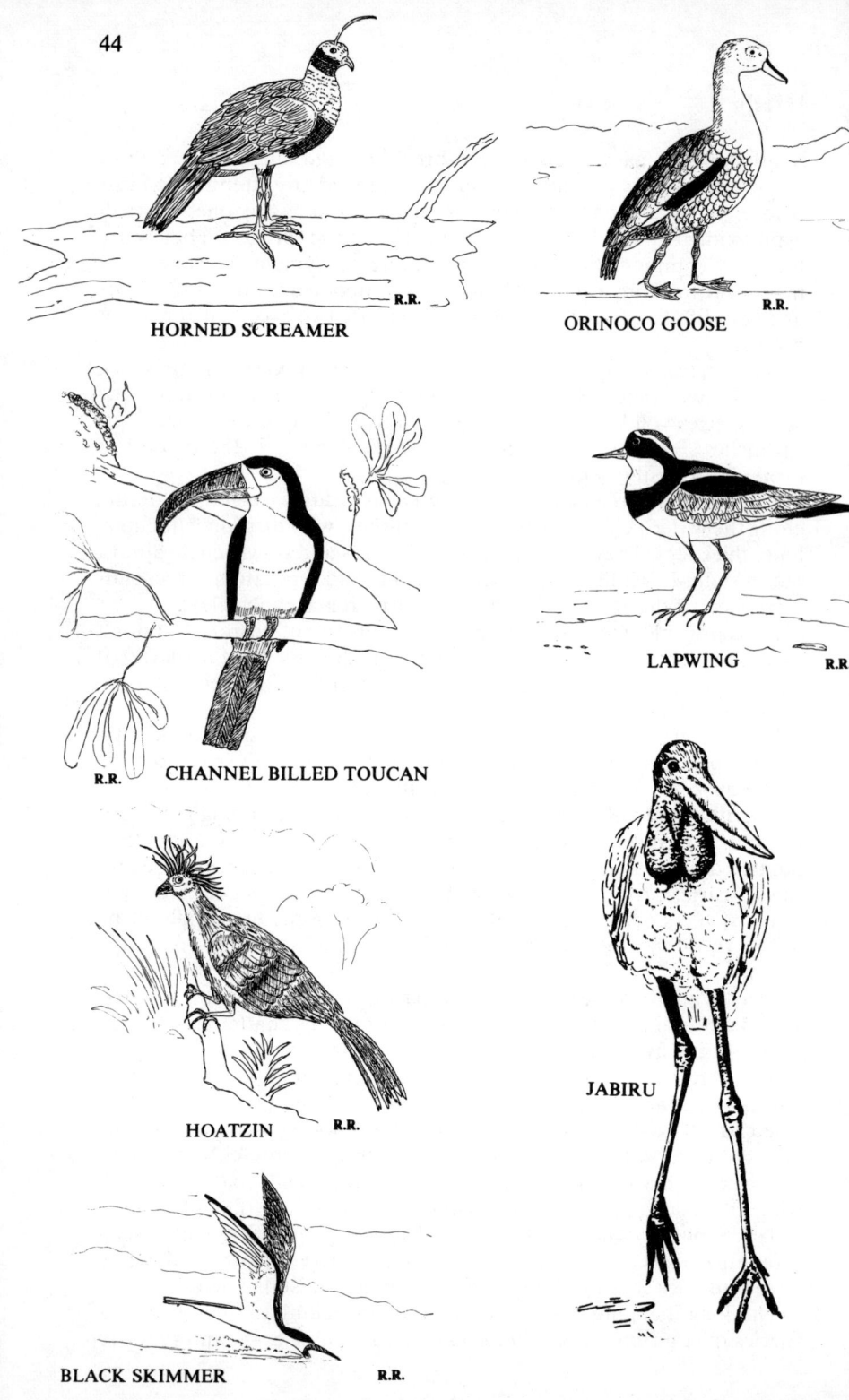

as large as crows, or no bigger than starlings. The **Yellow-rumped Cacique** (*Cacicus cela*) is 25 cm. long, and basically black with bright yellow on the lower back, rump and tail-base. It has a long sharp lemon-yellow bill and blue eyes and the reputation for being the most musical of all colonial nesting birds. Their variety of songs and calls are both beautiful and funny. And notice dozens of birds, all clinging to their nests, bowing, shaking their tails and wings while other birds dart among the nests. After the male weaves the nest he must attract a mate, which explains all the frantic displaying and house viewing.

Two terns are regularly seen on the rivers. The **Yellow-billed Tern** (*Sterna superciliaris*) is small (23–27 cm.) and delicate with a deeply forked white tail and sporting black wing tips and cap. The **Large-billed Tern** (*Phaetusa simplex*) is distinguished by a thick, oversized yellow bill and three distinctive wing bars. The tail is short, and shallowly notched.

Swooping for insects over rivers you will usually see the **White-banded Swallow** (*Atticora fasciata*) with deeply forked tail and broad banded breast, along with the **White-winged Swallow** (*Tachycineta albiventer*) which is glossy-green and looks like a butterfly.

On sandbars you will see **Pied Lapwings** (*Hoploxypterus cayanus*). They're dressed in such contrasting black and white they appear to be head waiters, but they have sporty red legs and scarlet eye-shadow. The other common plover, the **Collared** (*Charadrius collaris*), is comparatively plain.

Since it is partially nocturnal you will see the **Black Skimmer** (*Rynchops niger*) most often resting on sandbars with all heads in the flock pointing in the same direction. The most unforgettable sight on jungle rivers is watching skimmers feed. They fly gracefully over the water, their long lower mandibles plowing below the surface catching small fish.

If you land on a sandbar you might stir up a group of **Sand-colored Nighthawks** (*Chordeiles rupestris*) so perfectly camouflaged they're almost impossible to see against the sand. When airborne you can appreciate their delicate coloring: streaks and spots of buff, white and blackish-brown break up their sandy color. Tails are long and forked with white outer feathers.

The **Hoatzin** (*Opisthocomus hoazin*) is the strangest bird you will ever see. Though common in the Amazon basin, you must make a special effort to find them. Your efforts should be rewarded by a glimpse of a modern throwback to Jurassic lizard-birds, the **archaeopteryx**, living two hundred million years ago.

If you find a primeval looking swamp or lake stop and search for Hoatzins. These big, sedentary, and lazy birds roost in large flocks. Just after dawn, and before sunset, they clamor about making loud hoarse cries and hissing. In the hot part of the day they rest in dense undergrowth. They are pheasant-like in appearance, about 65 cm. long, with broad tails. Their plumage is brownish-green, spotted with white. Their habitat and disproportionately small head distinguish them from other birds. Flying is limited to awkward forays across small creeks, or launching themselves from treetops. Wings are used mainly for balance.

Young Hoatzins, not being any more agile than their parents, often fall into the water under their nests. Luckily, chicks have the ability to swim well, and claws on their shoulders allow them to climb out of the water and back up the tree to their nest.

The **Sunbittern** (*Eurypyga helias*) is a graceful, quiet bird about 45 cm. long seen foraging along muddy shores. Sunbitterns superficially resemble herons but are easily distinguished by their long tails, and intricate bars and speckles in many shades of brown, rufous and gray. When spread, the wings sport two round chestnut suns.

In the middle of the day you will see herons and storks and even a spoonbill. Along with the abundant **Snowy Egret** (*Egretta thula*), easily recognized by bright yellow feet contrasting with black legs, look for the large **White-necked Heron** (*Ardea cocoi*). Similar to the temperate **Great Blue Heron,** this bird is gray-black with a forehead, crown, and crest of black.

The **Capped Heron** (*Pilherodius pileatus*) is much smaller, nearly all white with a yellowish tinge on its neck, black crown and blue bill. A solitary, shy bird it is difficult to approach to see its delicate markings.

Two storks you will want to identify are the **Jaribu** (*Jabiru mycteria*) and the **Wood Stork** (*Mycteria americana*). The former is 130 cm. tall, and all white except for a bare black head and neck. Its heavy black bill is slightly upturned. In contrast, the **Wood Stork** is shorter, with a downturned bill.

In flight herons and storks are easily distinguishable: herons fly with their necks pulled back, while storks fully extend their necks.

The adult **Roseate Spoonbill** (*Ajaia ajaja*), 85 cm., is pink with some crimson on the shoulders. Immature birds may be only tinged with pink, but the spoonbill in any plumage can be recognized by its long, flat bill broadened and rounded at the tip. Spoonbills wade in shallow water while they feed, moving their open bills rapidly from side to side beneath the surface to catch various forms of aquatic life.

The small (15 cm.) stout big-headed blackish birds seen along the rivers, perched in pairs in the tops of naked trees, are **Swallow-wings** (*Chelidoptera tenebrosa*), one of the puffbirds. They dart from the treetops snatching insects from the air. Their bills are thick at the base, sharp and downcurved at the end. In flight their shape can be mistaken for a bat or swallow. Their nests are burrowed in the ground.

Guans, Currasows, and **Chachalacas** comprise a group of birds known as *Cracidae*. They are big birds, many as large as turkeys. The jungles are full of them, but they are usually heard and not seen. Most of these species cannot be identified unless they are seen clearly. If you see them at all, it will likely be only a glimpse. On a seldom-traveled river you could luck upon one of these birds in full view at a clearing at the water's edge. More often, you will see only their dark silhouettes in the trees. They wear curly crests, wattles, helmets, or other strange protuberances on their heads. Take careful note of all the markings should you see one at close range as they are maddeningly similar.

Guans are arboreal, while currasows forage on the ground. All *Cracidae* are vegetarian and some are noisy, particularly chachalacas, whose name is derived from their raucous cackling which once heard will never be forgotten.

Toucans are wonderful to see; don't worry about trying to identify them. There are thirty-seven species of toucans, varying in size from 30 to 60 cm. The long tailed, middle-sized, or small ones are usually aracaris. Toucans have enormous bills, sometimes longer than their bodies, and almost equal to it in bulk. Generally, their bills have patches of several bright, contrasting colors, as do their bodies. To sort out these various patterns you must see a toucan sitting quietly. But you are more likely to see them flapping and gliding across the river. Once in the trees toucans are difficult to spot from a boat, but on shore you may get a closer look at them: they are curious about you too so they allow you near. Toucans are frolicsome and amusing while feeding. Their long bills were intended perhaps to reach for fruit on the tips of twigs while perched on a stable branch. But if you see a group feeding you will notice many swaying limbs and tipping toucans.

The **Swallow-tailed Kite** (*Elanoides forficatus*) is one of the most beautiful and graceful birds in the Amazon basin. This 65 cm. hawk cannot be confused because of its long, deeply forked tail as it glides and soars over the treetops like no other bird. Its head and entire underbody are white, contrasting with its back, wings and tail which are glossy black.

The **King Vulture** (*Sarcorhamphus papa*) is particularly striking, it is the only predominately white vulture, and has a wing-span of about 2 m. When soaring you will see black on the end of the tail and trailing half of its wings.

Even rarer is the **Harpy Eagle** (*Harpia harpyja*) standing at 1 m., with a 2 m. wing-span, it is probably the strongest bird of prey in the world. The female, larger than the male, can weigh up to 7 kilos. These eagles eat monkeys, coatis and other mammals as well as other birds. It has a black back and a white underside, with a broad black band on its neck that disappears under its wings. Its long black tail has four gray bands.

Wildlife Viewing

The various trips in this book cover almost 3,200 km. of latitude, spanning all of South America except the last 1,400 km. Most of this book describes rivers within the tropical and subtropical belts. It is within these areas that the greatest number of animals and birds flourish.

They are not easily viewed as most live in the jungle canopy, but traveling by river is probably the most likely method of seeing a broad variety of animals and birds. Here are a few ideas about viewing wildlife.

ON LAND

Contrary to popular belief the equatorial rain forest, The Jungle, is not impenetrable. Conditions on the forest floor do not favor development of undergrowth, and these same conditions inhibit animal development as well.

However, by walking (along creeks, swamps and lakes) is the best way to see the few ground dwelling animals of the Amazon basin during the dry season. Often, by staying still, animals will be heard rustling among the leaves looking for fallen fruits, blossoms and nuts. If you have the time and patience, pitch your mosquito netting near water, or fallen fruit, and watch the action.

Subtropical forests are lower, with a more open canopy. This allows more sunlight to reach the earth and causes luxurient, impenetrable vegetation to flourish. Many animals and birds find shelter here. It is possible to cut your way through this type of forest, but do not underestimate the time needed to do so. Cutting a trail wide enough for comfortable passage by people with loads is hard work and six kilometers daily would be considered wonderful progress in dense jungle.

Unfortunately the noise made by cutting a trail scares off animals or birds you hope to see, but on succeeding days quiet passage along the trail may reveal interesting sights, as jungle life returns. Often it is possible to avoid this work by searching for an already cut trail. Ask your guide, or the locals, about this possibility.

You might consider walking across a river loop, between two parts of the same river. Obviously the more loops your river makes the shorter your walk will be. Often the growth in such an area is not difficult to get through; however you may find many old trees, roots and deep mud impede your progress.

FROM THE RIVER

Your view of the riverbank from any sort of craft on the river will consist of beach backed by a succession of grasses, bushes and finally jungle canopy. This general scene is called the galleria, and is home for most of the area's birds and animals. An inspection of the beach and grassy areas will reveal a myriad of bird and animal tracks: pacca, deer, agouti, tapier and jaguar.

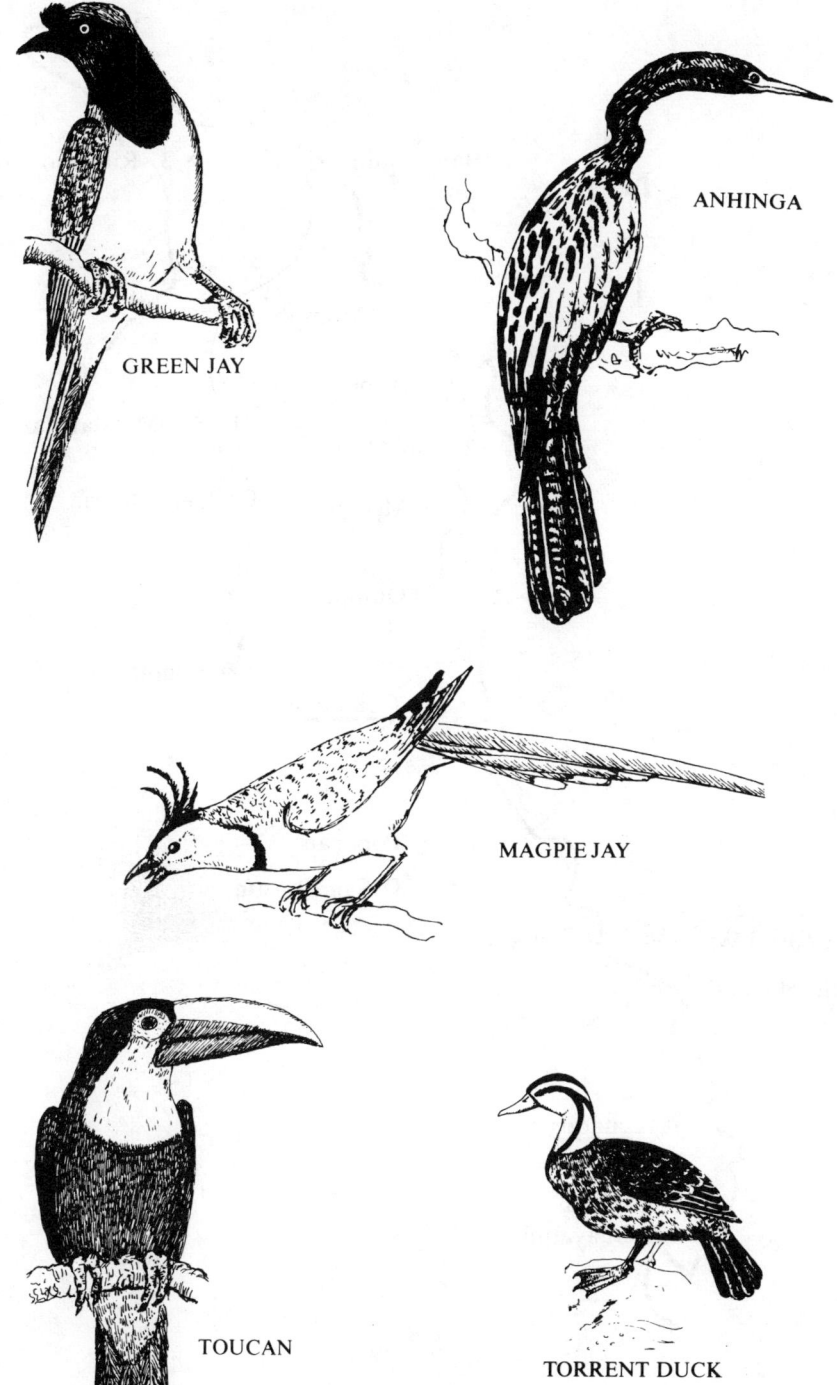

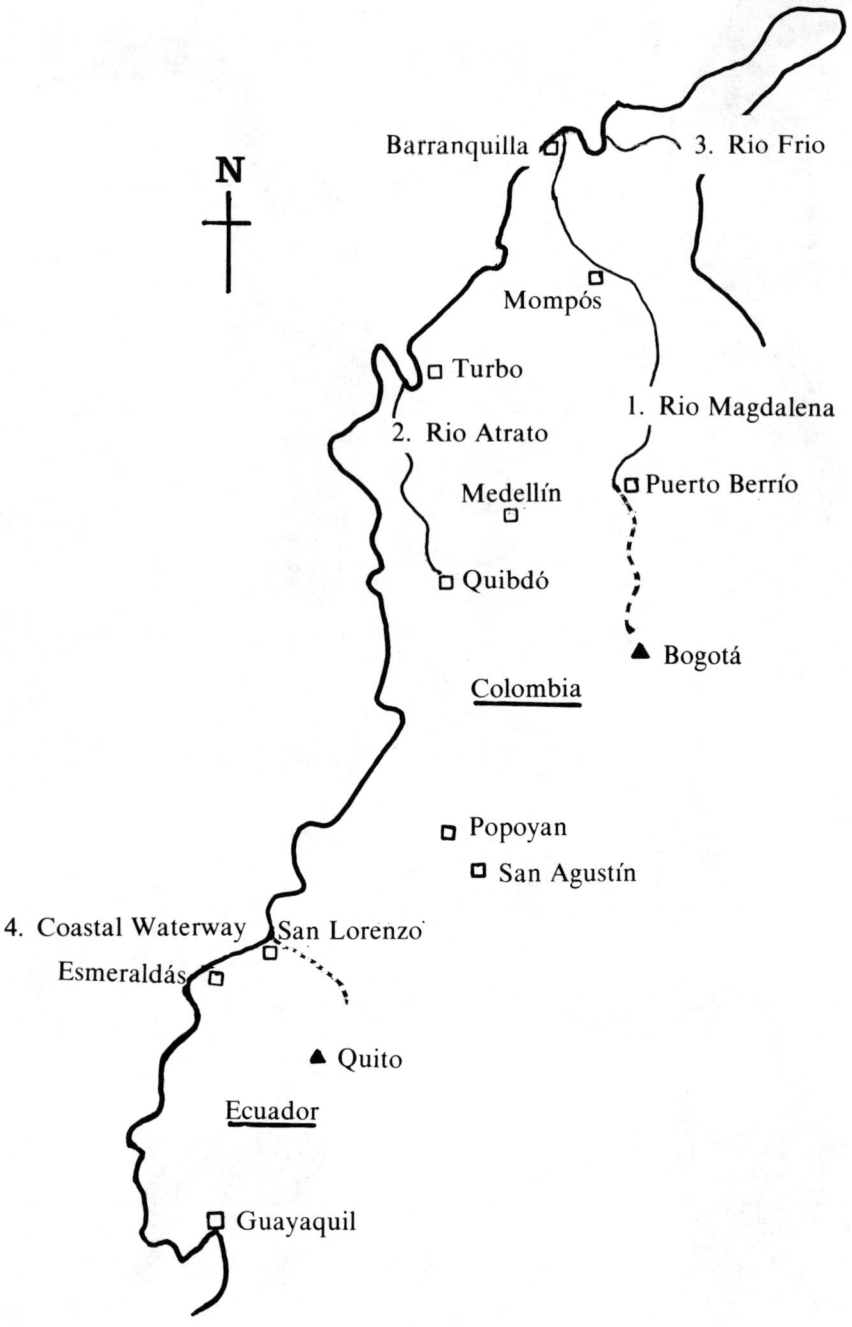

V Rivers

North of the Amazon

FACT BOX

Country: Colombia

River: Magdalena

Embarkation Points: Many between Puerto Berrío & Mompós
  Type of Craft: Motorized Canoes, Speedboats
  Time & Distance: Entire section between Puerto Berrío & Mompós 400 km. but many short hops are possible

Connections:
  Trains and buses run along the river, stopping at most of the embarkation points.

Options:
  Speeding on the Magdalena, packed into commuter boats, may not be your idea of fun, but unfortunately most of the old side-wheeler steamboats are disappearing from service.
  The opportunity to travel by boat, bus and train all in one day may be attraction enough for some travelers.
  On certain sections of the river you may only be able to proceed if you hire an entire boat. Wherever you are on the river you'll find this service is not cheap or well organized. Beware of boatmen who promise express service; probably you'll be paying for all the empty seats so he can leave the dock sooner.
  The area is dry from December through April.

> This information has been provided by Dan Buck, a frequent contributor to **SOUTH AMERICAN EXPLORER MAGAZINE.**

FACT BOX

Country: Colombia, NW

River: Atrato

Embarkation Points: Quibdó—Turbo
  Type of Craft: Cargo Boats
  Classes & Costs: Hammock—$25
  Time & Distance 4–5 Days, 200 km.

Connections:
  Bus: From Medellín: 12–15 hours
  Air: From Medellín: 1 hour
  Rail: Not possible

Options:
  Day trip to Necocli (50 km. north of Turbo) for glimpses of Cuna Indians; swimming; and a relaxed atmosphere.

  From Turbo there are usually night crossings to Puerto Obaldia if you want to then cross into Panama. The trip is apt to be a rough and crowded one, and the journey on to Panama City long and expensive. Making the crossing via the Darien Gap (fully described in *Backpacking in Mexico & Central America*) is much easier.

Rio Atrato By George Bradt

Part I: Medillin—Quibdó

With luck the 240 km. trip between Medillín and Quibdó takes twelve hours. It is a wonderfully scenic road, crossing two mountain chains, but it is very dusty in the dry season. During the wet season (from March through October) there is no dust, but the road is so bad the trip could take two or three days.

As the trip begins the bus is loaded with various shades of white people, but as it progresses toward Quibdó the whites are replaced by blacks. Seemingly, Chocó Province is run by a totally black administration often at odds with the central government in Bogotá.

We arrived in Quibdó just after dark and were welcomed by many friendly people. In the dark, coated with a thick layer of dust, we must have looked acceptable. A small boy escorted us to a large wooden hotel perched high on the riverbank. The hotel was aglow with candlelight. From our window we could see candles and flashlight beams floating through the soft darkness down by the river.

"Everything's fine. Now please show us the shower."

The boy laughed and pointed out the window toward the river. We asked why and were told, "No hay gasolina." We allowed this small but significant fact to seep into our minds. Our worst fears were confirmed by learning that gasoline usually arrives by boat.

Next morning we looked out and saw twenty cargo boats tipped crazily in the shallows. Before riding all the way back to Medellín we thought we'd sample Quibdó's delights. Certainly swimming in the river was one of them as was talking to the friendly people. We saw a family of Indians from a remote tributary on their way to the local missionary's house for free medical attention. We decided to tag along, perhaps discussing our travel prospects with the missionary would be instructive. We were determined to find a way of swapping apparent defeat for some sort of victory in any possible way. We arrived at his office in time to see the missionary pulling a bullet out of an Indian's arm.

When the Indians had gone the missionary gave us the benefit of his undivided attention. To every elaborate idea of ours he replied only, "No, it's impossible." When we ran out of ideas he suggested taking the bus back to Medellín.

We did hear of one couple who got to Quibdó after the rains had begun. They waited patiently for enough water and for the cargo (bananas) to be loaded. No sooner had they boarded and cast off when their boat overturned. Fortunately nobody was hurt, but the gringos were so shaken, they too went back to Medellín.

Part II: Medellín—Turbo

There's a bus every day between Medellín and Turbo; it's a 13 hour trip down to the Caribbean port. There are also planes twice or three times weekly. Once in Turbo you can inquire around the port (in the middle of town) for boats going upriver. How far they go depends on how much water there is, but there is at least one boat every day.

We went up to Sautatá, where the headquarters for the *Los Katios* National Park are located. The trip only takes 5 hours; we saw monkeys, parrots and a toucan. The national park is a fascinating place with many birds, but officially you need permission to enter the park and stay at the headquarters in Sautatá. The permission is obtained in the I.N.D.E.R.E.N.A. office in Medellín. They will serve meals and allow you a bunk, but conditions are primitive.

It might be possible to get a boat from Turbo going up to Puerto Libre (just beyond Sautatá) and back in the same day.

Rio Frio Serendipity

By Joseph Rosenbloom III

The idea of a South American river adventure never occurred to me until I was in South America and close to the river. Then I agreed to an excursion on the Rio Frio in Colombia for the same reason the chicken crossed to the other side of the road. The chicken came to the road and crossed it. I came to the Rio Frio and ventured onto it.

I would prefer a more ennobling explanation. I would prefer to report that I had felt a gnawing desire to explore the Rio Frio since, say, that exhilarating day in sixth grade when I almost choked with delight in perusing pictures of the river in the *National Geographic.* I would prefer to report that I had: A. read everything I could get my hands on about the flora and fauna of the Rio Frio; B. planned for years something on the scale of the Lewis-and-Clark expedition; and C. saved and scrimped to acquire a Boston Whaler and a Nikon F3 camera preparatory to a serious jungle endeavor.

The truth is sadly otherwise. I went to Colombia intent to stay on the beach and work assiduously on a suntan. Toward that end, I had joined a friend, Bill Henry, on an American Express package tour to Colombia. The tour entitled us to a week in the country, with stops at the Caribbean cities of Cartagena and Santa Marta.

The possibility of an excursion on the Rio Frio—indeed, the very existence of the Rio Frio—penetrated into my sun-baked brain only toward the end of the vacation. We were staying at the Irotama Hotel near Santa Marta. We happened upon a notice posted in the hotel tourist office advertising a one-day outing on the river.

Henry liked the idea better than I. "If we've come all this way," he said, "we really ought to see a patch of jungle." What iced it for me was the Marquez connection. As a sole concession to seriousness of purpose, I had dragged along on vacation with me a novel, *One Hundred Years of Solitude,* by the famed Gabriel Garcia Marquez. He was born in Aracataca, a town located in the river basin of which the Rio Frio is a part. 'Here is my chance to see a bit of Marquez country,' I thought as I signed on for the excursion to the Rio Frio.

The Rio Frio is part of a network of rivers in northernmost Colombia that flow from the Santa Marta mountains to the Caribbean. On a map the rivers look like the fingers of a hand dangling into the sea.

To reach the Rio Frio, we drove first by bus to the edge of a vast lake, the Cienaga Grande. There we climbed into a long, wooden dugout that could have passed for a genuine stone age artifact except for the outboard motor mounted on the stern. Overhead, to shield us from the sun, there was a bamboo mat on poles like the roof of a surrey.

In the early morning, the lake was a shimmering expanse of astounding beauty, and remarkable depth; fishermen stood alongside dugouts casting their nets in long, graceful arcs. On the lake we saw cormorants, herons, storks and cranes, to mention only the birds we could identify. Startled by the outboard, the birds scooted away from us with much flapping and squawking.

It took more than an hour to reach the mouth of the Rio Frio. Suddenly, the dugout turned into the current. The banks on both sides of the river, maybe as wide apart as a football field, were clogged with trees and vegetation. I stuck my hand into the water to see whether the river deserved its name. The water felt cool, but not really cold.

Before long, we saw our first troop of monkeys. They seemed oblivious to us, as they scampered high in the trees. A bit further, we spotted a dead crocodile floating sluggishly in the water. He seemed oblivious to us, too.

A few minutes later we heard a distant wail, "That's a jaguar," our guide Rogelio said excitedly. We never saw the jaguar. But Rogelio assured us the jungle has many jaguars, scorpions and tarantulas, among other creatures. "Not everyone who walks into the jungle walks out of the jungle," Rogelio said. No one contradicted him.

We followed Rogelio's advice and ate our sandwiches in the dugout before heading back to the lake. We traveled a half hour until we reached a village of thatched huts standing on stilts over the water. Dark-skinned children, some naked, rushed from the huts to greet us. Rogelio responded by throwing little balls of hard-rock candy at the children. They eupted into a frenzy. "Bolas, bolas," they shrieked, some of them plunging into the water to swim after the dugout.

We stopped, briefly, at a rickety landing in the center of the village. I particularly remember one little boy, maybe eight years old, who pointed in consternation at my eyeglasses and watched in disbelief as I put suntan oil on my arm, then insisted that I put some on his arm.

Henry asked to use the lavatory. It consisted of a hole cut in wooden planks over the water. Down below, a great school of carp waited expectantly amidst a latticework of algea. As we left the village, Rogelio explained that the inhabitants live both on the edge of the jungle and on the edge of starvation. They suffer from amoebic dysentery, pneumonia and numerous other diseases, our guide informed us.

Later, back in the hotel room, I read more of the Marquez novel. "To the south," he writes, referring to the Colombian interior, "lay the swamps, covered with an eternal vegetable scum, and the whole vast universe of the great swamp, which, according to what the gypsies said, had no limits."

Still mulling it all over, I decided to return to the beach for just a little more sunshine before the plane left for New York.

> The best hammocks made in South America are Colombian. We've met people who have looked all over Peru, in vain, for a hammock. Mexico also makes fine hammocks, if you are passing through on your way south. But if you are flying directly into the Amazon basin, and doing a hammock-class river trip you should buy a hammock at home.

FACT BOX

Country: Ecuador, NW

River: Coastal Waterway—Pacific Ocean

Embarkation Points: Quito, Esmeraldas, La Tola, San Lorenzo, Ibarra
 Type of Craft: Motorized Canoes
 Classes & Costs: Day trip, $7
 Time & Distance: 3 Hours, 50 km.

Connections:
 Train: San Lorenzo—Ibarra 7 hr.
 Bus: Ibarra—La Tola via Esmeraldas & Quito 11 hr.
 Boat: La Tola—San Lorenzo 3 hr.

Options:
 This is a loop trip, start anywhere, end anywhere. Not only do you travel by three different modes, but you see every life-zone of the slopes of the western Andes. It is a fascinating trip. Allow two whole days, minimum, to complete the loop.

Esmeraldas Coastal Waterway   By Marc Dubin

For travelers planning to visit both Otavalo and Esmeraldas this route is an ideal way to avoid passing several times through Quito. The water trip is only about three hours, but that's really all you would want in the gray, green mangrove maze between La Tola and San Lorenzo. These swamps are well traveled, with lots of canoes whose pilots vary in age, sex, and garb. The sky and channels abound with hundreds of noisy pelicans fishing and diving. Some of the passageways through the mangrove swamps are so narrow that tree branches dangle into the boat. At other points along the muddy shoreline you'll see one or two *casas montuvias* (houses above the rains) or whole towns of them.

The *Cooperativa La Costenita* runs *chivos* (open-sided bus-trucks) from Esmeraldas to La Tola daily at 7 am. and 11 am. (same schedule returning). The dirt road passes flat deserted beaches, fishing villages and coconut groves. After four hours on the truck the passengers embark in canoes for San Lorenzo, leaving at noon and 4 pm. The 8 meter craft, each crammed with at least 20 passengers, never gets near the open sea (fortunately) but keeps to the brackish inland waterway system. Limones, 50 minutes from La Tola, is the ocean port of the Esmeraldas River, and there's usually a boat or two unloading cargo. At Tambio, the halfway mark, there is a brief stop. It is a village on wooden stilts, boardwalks and a forest of TV antennas. After another ninety minutes you arrive in San Lorenzo.

San Lorenzo is a sleepy friendly town with not much to do. If you plan to leave the next day your priority should be making a reservation on the train for Ibarra. San Lorenzo is a good base for visiting the Cayapas Indians who live up the Cayapas River.

There is a terrific marimba band in San Lorenzo. Because the band has been ripped off by recording and filming agencies, it is best to visit Carlos Rubio, the band's director, who lives in a blue corner house one block from the train station. He'll be able to tell you the band's schedule of rehearsals, usually held in the Hotel Imperial near the canoe office.

Two trains daily leave at 6 am. and 1 pm. for Ibarra. The train, a rickety *autoferro*, stops for a meal at Lita (about halfway) and is besieged by vendors at Carchi, two hours from Ibarra.

From San Lorenzo to Lita is a 1,500 m. climb through rain forest with occasional views of the foaming Rios Mira and Lita. Between Lita and Carachi (2,500 m.) the terrain gradually dries up. Beyond Carachi the track winds through the badlands of the Chota watershed and then suddenly levels out at the oasis of Salinas. Between Salinas and Ibarra two or three *nevados*, including Volcan Cayambe (5,790 m.), can be seen in clear weather.

From Ibarra it's just a short hop on one of the many buses to Quito.

A sheet sleeping bag, just an ordinary sheet sewn across the bottom and up the side, is useful for the tropics. Often it is all that is needed at night, and it offers protection against scratchy woolen blankets should the weather turn cool. Doubled on the bottom of your hammock it offers added protection against mosquitos.

Bluet Gaz, a French manufacturer, makes a small stove running on cartridges of pressurized gas. They have two models, both widely distributed in North America and Europe, but the smaller of the two is called the Globetrotter. The stove, and cartridge, fit neatly into two pots which come with a handle. This outfit would be very handy on a river trip, however you are traveling, for a quick cup of tea, bouillon or warming up those canned supplies you've purchased. The small cartridges are not yet widely distributed in South America, so bring some with you, without telling the airlines.

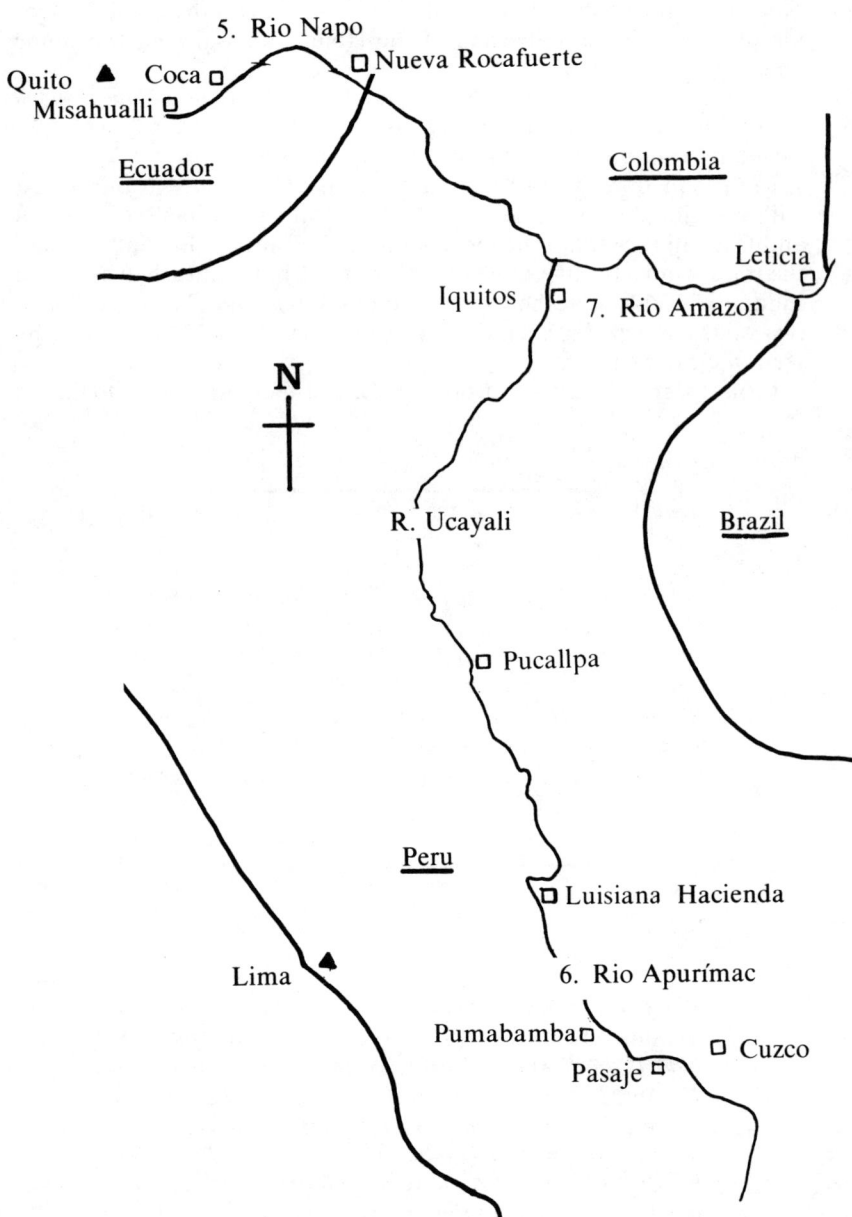

Amazon Basin: North, West, South

FACT BOX

Country: Ecuador, SE

River: Napo

Embarkation Points: Coca—Misahuallí
  Type of Craft: Motorized Canoes
  Time & Distance: 1 Day, 100 km., $15

Connections:
  Bus from Quito via Lago Agrio, or via Baños
  About 18 hours, 325 km. either way

Options:
  Four day hike to Auca Indian villages.
  Exploring the jungle around the Hotel Jaguar which is two hours downriver from Misahuallí (Reservations: Quito 239400).
  Going on to Puerto Nueva Rocafuerte, on the border with Peru. Chances of getting down to Iquitos slim. River travel between border and Iquitos prohibited, only one plane weekly.

The Rio Napo   By George Bradt

The thrill of feeling our boat being pushed off the riverbank, out into the caramel-colored Napo was exciting. From this spot, high in the Ecuadorian jungle, the Rio Napo flows northeast, then jags into Peru and joins the Amazon just downstream from Iquitos.

Because the river was narrow we were able to scan every meter of shore for wildlife and each midstream snag was inspected for birdlife. As we headed into each riverbend our field-glasses were trained on the shore to catch sight of any animal before the sound of our engine frightened it into flight. Despite our best efforts we saw nothing but a few common river birds.

It was fun feeling the currents as our 12 m. dugout slashed through the eddies and backwaters, the boat pitching and yawing. Now that we were watching the river instead of the shore we were amazed we hadn't tipped over or shipped water. The dugout seemed unsteady, but responsive to the motor. Ahead came an undulating backbone of waves, created by the river squeezing through enormous boulders. We took a deep breath and gripped the gunwales. There was no other way through this gullet of rock and surf; we were both tense with the same awareness. Suddenly we were through it; not half as bad as it looked. We glanced around at the motorman, he waved, grinned and gave us the thumbs up sign.

His assistant now stood in the bow directing the motorman with arm and hand movements, the current frothing and surging in midstream 10 km/h. Our own speed, about 25 km/h., combined with typical latin bravado, didn't allow any room for miscalculation. The least indecision, a wide turn, or an excess of speed: disaster.

Occasionally the river became too shallow for the motor, so it was slowed and hoisted out of the water as we skidded over the rocks. During these interludes the boat was completely at the river's mercy; fortunately the Napo took good care of us, along with the motorman.

Ahead we could see a set of shallow rapids, no big rocks, just a white frill across the river from shore to shore, then the river deepened into a turn and went around an island. By now we were enjoying the anticipation of the motorman's moves, but this was a tricky situation: how would we make the turn with the motor out of the water?

Time would tell, but we were already halfway through the riffled water and approaching the turn. The bowman was signaling, but the motorman could do nothing as long as the engine was out of the water. The riffles ended as the water deepened. The engine pushed back into the water and the canoe sped away from the island. But the bowman saw something ahead and signaled to turn back. Panic! The bank!

The motor screamed and died as everything went green and crashing. Leaning forward and holding our ankles, we hoped for the best. The noises gradually subsided as the boat halted, held by a tangle of branches. We looked at each other, whole, in amazed good fortune. When we looked for the motorman there was nothing to see except green. Silence. We were relieved when he started shouting out of the greenery at the bowman. Everyone was fine. We pushed the boat from under the foliage and set off again toward midstream.

An hour later the engine slowed as we banked across the river and glided up a quiet tributary. With the motor burring we passed under a high, leafy canopy of silent jungle on water as black as muddy coffee. All too soon we tied up along several other canoes and mounted the bank into a rough clearing. The scant afternoon light revealed a small house, our home for the night.

The clearing looked new and tenuous surrounded by vigorous jungle and enormous trees. They were tall and straight, with an evenly shaped umbrella of leaves and branches close to the top. The massive trunks, covered in smooth, grey bark, stood on roots that formed buttresses curving out from the ground. Around one giant we noticed that fins had been converted into natural cages for animals. Each compartment, closed by a mat of woven bullrushes, contained a new and interesting group of livestock: river turtles, small rodents, chickens, etc. We felt like Swiss Family Robinson, marooned on our island in the jungle. A flock of parrots shrieked overhead on their way home for the night.

As darkness fell, marvelous smells began wafting our way from the cooking hut that separated the sleeping quarters. We would dine on turtle and yucca. We could hardly wait; finally the meal arrived on banana leaves with large mounds of rice. Delicious. After everyone had eaten their fill and had coffee, we all stretched out on the floor and fell instantly to sleep.

At dawn it was raining. After a leisurely breakfast we left. It rained all the way to Coca. Scrambling up the slippery steps, cut into the muddy bank, was a real challenge. But even a dunking wouldn't have made much difference; nothing would have dampened our memories of the river and the generous people we met.

> Nights along a river are misty, even under a perfectly clear sky. The river stays warm while the land cools rapidly once the sun sets; the imbalance creates a mist.
> Not only will mist saturate anything absorbent, it will seriously rust and corrode any metal except enamel and aluminum. Remember always to cover items left outside at night.

walbro water purifier

P mac
MARKETING INTERNATIONAL
1320 36th Ave., San Francisco, CA 94122

(415) 564-0506

Published annually in November, the encyclopaedic
South American Handbook
including the Caribbean, Mexico and Central America.
Nearly 1,300 pages with 8 pp. colored sectional maps.

"The best guidebook on South America"

Available from your bookstore, or direct from
Trade & Travel Publications, Bath, England.

FACT BOX

Country: Peru, SE
River: Apurímac
Embarkation Points: Pumabamba, Cunyoc, Pasaje
  Type of Craft: Rubber Raft
  Cost: See Outfitters List, under Back Country International
  Time and Distance: Variable between two days and five.

The Rio Apurímac: Source of the Amazon

By John Tichenor

Thousands of rivers join to form the Amazon, carrying rainwater that originally fell on every conceivable type of landscape in South America. Most of these rivers are born in the jungle, or just above it, on the rain-drenched eastern slope of the Andes. They cascade immediately to the Amazon basin and flow through the jungle all the way to the Atlantic. A separate group of tributaries rises in the interior valleys of the Andes and flows north, lengthwise through the great mountain chains forming the Andes. Before finally combining as the Amazon in northern Peru these rivers carve through an unparalleled spectrum of geography: glaciers, grassland villages, agricultural valleys and desert canyons. Many villagers living along the rivers simply don't believe that these streams eventually join the Amazon, if indeed they have ever heard of the Amazon. Accordingly, local names often change with the geography; each section is a separate world, an isolated bit of time and life unknowingly tied to the mightiest river on earth.

Of all the mountain tributaries, perhaps the most remote and remarkable is the Rio Apurímac, the source of the Amazon. The river is born in an icy canyon in southern Peru, just 150 km. east of the Pacific Ocean. A journey of six thousand kilometers lies ahead, most of it jungle river. But in the first tenth of the trip the Apruímac cascades through an incredible descent from ice to altiplano and has carved an immense desert canyon nearly 3,000 meters deep.

The canyon separated northern cultures from the developing empires near Lake Titicaca and Cuzco. But the militant Incas spanned the chasm with a famous woven suspension bridge and opened the way for their northern conquests. The name Apu-rimac means 'Lord Oracle' and the river lord was often consulted by high-ranking Incas as they passed the canyon. A special town was built to maintain the fiber bridge and to guard the effigy symbolizing the Oracle.

We found the magic of the Apurímac was concentrated in the 100 km. between the high, cold mountains and warm, subtropical Amazonia. Because the entire transition unfolds within such a short distance a wide variety of ecological zones, comprised of many small niches, were crammed together in unique and stunning combinations. Here nature was trying out new ideas and varieties of adaptability. Those which adapted successfully moved elsewhere and continued their development until climate changes bring a new, better adapted species. Nature abhors all vacuums, however brief, everywhere.

We explored the Apurímac in three parts on three separate trips between 1977 and 1979. The first of these began at the bridge of Cunyoc, where the river runs wide and lazy for a few kilometers, then twists into a narrow gorge full of cascades. There were some beautiful moments on this trip; but after many portages and prospects of more, we were glad to leave the canyon. We packed out to the village of Cachora and returned to Cuzco.

The second exploration went very well. We started further downstream and avoided the heaviest cascades. We entered the canyon at Pasaje, after a steep one day descent. The canyon is still 2,500 meters deep, but it's shaped like a V instead of an exclamation point. From Pasaje the river ran through the familiar pattern of grand canyon rapids, and we screamed with delight through white water and rolling waves. At night there were white sand beaches and sunbaked rocks to lie on and gaze at the stars.

We reached Pumabamba in three days and a single portage. This was where we left the river and headed back to Cuzco.

The only problem we had was the sandflies; they were voracious. But we soon discovered they wouldn't fly over water so all day we were comfortable. They were no trouble after sunset, but with the first light we had to be up and packing because the beasts awoke. Any exposed flesh was targeted for bites, with ankles and ears earning an extra share. Fortunately both repellent and clothing were effective deterrents, but the best escape was always toward water. We made a point of getting off to early starts.

On our third trip on the Apurímac, we put in at Pumabamba. The river had surprises for us, but most of them were incredibly pleasant. Jim caught trout for breakfast, breezes were gentle most of the day, and the flies that had plagued us upstream were easy to avoid. Rolling swells and sparkling rapids welcomed us back to the river as we glided downstream again. In the long pools between rapids the canyon was quiet with almost a cathedral air—the bare, vertical walls seemed to turn about us and lean toward each other. Sculpted granite arched in abstract alcoves, and like most sunny cathedrals there were swallows nesting in the high corners.

Three long turns and a rolling rapid whistled by before we reached the falls at Pawac. Paddling ashore for a look, we found the entire river racing through a gap less than eight meters wide, and bouncing through a double wave to the pool below. Under less remote circumstances it might have been fun to run, but we quickly voted for the conservative option and portaged.

Two hours later both rafts were loaded and ready to continue. A long set of rapids stretched out just downstream, so we pulled into the

APURÍMAC RIVER AT PASAJE–PERU, PHOTO: J. SILVA

current and crossed over for a better look from the opposite shore. Our landing was a grotto with a spring streaming down the deepest face, and a terrace filled with sandy hollows reached over the current below. It was so beautiful we made camp and spent the afternoon quietly reading, writing, and poking along the shore. Three boys spotted us from a trail above and brought down papayas and bananas to share. We feasted together and at dusk they ran home with a batch of cinnamon rolls left over from that morning's breakfast.

Crashing whitewater and swollen waves were first on the Apurímac menu the next morning, but by afternoon the roar had settled to a rumble. In the next four days the river's gradient gradually relaxed; rapids tumbled through the canyon each day, but mixed with longer stretches of quiet flow as the canyon disappeared. The cliffs above grew more verdant as they melted down to river level. First, ferns thickened on still vertical walls, then *agave* replaced the cactus and Spanish moss thrived as the air became moist. For nearly a full day the pending change was in the breeze, then in three quick turns of the river we were in jungle. The canyon still formed a gorge where trails couldn't follow, but the forest was rich and luxuriant. Weaverbirds and kingfishers slashed through the canyon and we spotted houses made of fronds instead of stone.

Even the geology changed. In the desert we drifted among granite boulders and cliffs of schist, but suddenly we were finding great masses of stone wadded together like honey buns in a bakery.

Waterfalls streamed through the forest and joined the Apurímac; the canyon walls alternately faded apart and squeezed together. The valley continually grew shallower, but it somehow grew more dramatic. Conversation was simply absorbed to create silence, the rafts drifted together, and rays of sunlight turned distinctly golden. The jungle seemed to pause and wait for the visitors to leave, parrots castigated us as we drifted away.

After three days of greening, the cliffs melted completely. The valley was marked only by widely spaced hills, although snowcapped peaks still loomed far behind us. The Apurímac drifted into a tropical homesteading region typical of upper Amazonia. Large tracts of jungle were now dotted with small farms raising fruit, cacao, and manioc root (the source of tapioca). The river widened to two hundred meters, monkeys scrambled in the forest canopy, and splashes of butterflies whirled along shore.

Finally, after five days on the river we arrived at the Hacienda Luisiana, a classic plantation harvesting sugarcane and converting it into rum for the highlanders. Trucks piled high with rum bottles left several times weekly. Since we were offered a ride up to Ayacucho we decided to accept and piled all our equipment on top of the rum bottles. The Apurímac was too busy becoming the Ene, Tambo, Ucayali and finally the Amazon to notice our departure.

Back Country International

THE PERU SPECIALISTS

Two routes lead to the remote corners of Peru: ancient trails through mountain meadows and backcountry villages; and rivers that surge where trails can't go. BackCountry International combines them both.

During the past five years BackCountry International has developed a series of predictably high quality trips at reasonable prices. These range from day trips rafting down the Sacred River of the Incas to a three week expedition which treks across Vilcabamba—then rafts down the ultimate source of the Amazon; from Grand Canyon whitewater to jungle meanders.

With us you can float past stone temples, hike Incan roads, sleep below a glacier, awake at Machu Picchu, dance at the Sun Festival, lunch with a farmer or fish for pirana where parrots scream overhead.

Journey Down the Amazon River

By Penny and Russell Jennings

Our journey toward the Amazon River began in Lima, Peru. We bought bus tickets for Pucallpa, a town on the Ucayali River. This river later becomes the Amazon. Pucallpa is the farthest town one can reach by road before having to travel the rivers. The bus tickets were bought from La Perla (Empresa de Transportes), Avenida 28 de Julio, 1529. From Lima to Pucallpa the distance is 840 km. We endured the bus journey for thirty hours, two flat tires, landslides and bogged roads. We traveled along gorges, over suspension bridges, past waterfalls and across flat terrain of Pampas del Sacramento.

We stayed in the Hotel Excelsior ($5.00 a double) located near the bus station where La Perla stops in Pucallpa. In the morning we enquired about river transport. We had to use Spanish. We were directed to the Port Captain's building, a grey building behind the market area. After learning that a boat, the *Campéon I*, would be leaving sometime during the day, we headed toward the port, a muddy embankment buzzing with activity. Cargo was being loaded and unloaded from various barges. Pigs and vultures quarrelled over scraps of garbage. The *Campéon I* would not be going, we were informed. We spent several hours making enquiries on boats and barges to find out who would be leaving and when and how much the fare would be. Some captains said the trip would last eight or nine days, others said five. Costs ranged from US$22.00 to $27.00 per person.

By midday we found a barge, the *R.M. Benevente* that would leave the following morning. Food was included in the fare of $22.00 whether we ate it or not. We had been advised by other travelers that the food prepared on board these boats was hazardous. We spent $27.00 on canned fruit, canned tuna fish, soda crackers, carrots, oranges, cans of juice and strawberry jam. After buying our food we returned to the boat to sleep on board. The boats tie up at the riverbank; there is no wharf.

When he saw us, the captain ordered two crew members to vacate a cabin. The cabin measured three metres by two metres. On the two bunks lay filthy, grease-stained mattresses. These we covered with brown wrapping paper. Greased pipes and chains protruded through the ceiling to the wheelhouse. When the helm was turned it moved the greasy chain through the ceiling and out through the floor. The chain spat grease. We covered it with newspaper.

We were the only foreigners on board. There were six other passengers who were going to their villages along the river.

The boat averaged 12 knots downriver. The Ucayali, very muddy, was one kilometer wide. Scrub and tall trees lined the banks. We passed villages of thatch roofed huts. We spotted dolphins. Mosquitos proved to be nuisances. Netting covered the window. We lit mosquito coils, slapped mosquito repellent on our exposed skin and sprayed the window netting. Even so, this was not 100% effective. During the trip we took PALUDRINE malaria tablets as they are the least toxic.

We stopped at large villages; the huts were of thatch but the shops were constructed with adobe bricks. Some shops had refrigerators, run on kerosene. The riverside Indian towns have schoolhouses and churches. The crew bought turtles to make soup. Bird and animal life was non-existent. Four and a half days after leaving Pucallpa we arrived in Iquitos.

We wanted to visit local Indian tribes. After exhaustive enquiries we booked with Amazon Safari Camp a two day, one night trip (24 hours, $31.00). We traveled along the Momon River, a minor tributary of the Amazon. We stayed in a rustic lodge. Rooms were clean with kerosene lanterns. The food was excellent: meat, potatoes, tamales (corn patties encased in pastry), tomatoes, dessert of pineapple, tea or coffee. The next day we were taken on a jungle walk to visit the villages of the Yagua and Jivaro Indians. They demonstrated their expertise with the blowgun. Our conclusion: the program was set up for tourists, but on reflection it was a rewarding experience.

There are Chinese stores in Iquitos' suburb of Belém. We bought hammocks ($12.00) and mosquito nets ($10.00).

For boats going downriver check *Agencia General de Representacions, Bermudez* 445. This building faces *Plaza 28 de Julio*. The office should know which boats are going. Check also the port at the end of Tawara West street. This is where we found a boat, the *Condessa*, that the *Agencia* did not know about. We paid $10.00 each for the four day trip to Ramon Castilla, Peru. Before leaving Iquitos, go to the Immigration office to get "stamped out" of Peru.

Green water-hyacinths and water-logged tree trunks floated down the river. On the banks tall trees, 30 metres high, intermittently rose above the scrub. Pineapples and bananas grow in gardens. Cows graze near the huts.

The boat took us to Ramon Castilla near where three borders meet: Peru, Colombia and Brazil. From Ramon Castilla we took a small motorboat across the river to Leticia (Colombia) where we stayed a few days. Tourism is highly organized here. You can visit Indian villages

FROM	TO	TRANSPORT	DURATION	DISTANCE	APPROX. COST
Lima............	Pucallpa	Bus	30 hours	840 km.	$ 18.00
Pucallpa.........	Iquitos	Barge	5 days	800 km.	$ 28.00
Iquitos..........	Ramon Castilla	Small Cargo boat	4 days	500 km.	$ 18.00
Ramon Castilla...	Leticia	Cross-river Ferry	¼ hour	2 km.	$ 3.00
Leticia.........	Benjamin Constant	Ferry	2 hours	10 km.	$ 2.00
Benjamin Constant	Manaus	Passenger boat	5 days	1,800 km.	$ 45.00
Manaus..........	Santarem	Ditto	2 days	450 km.	$ 20.00
Santarem........	Belém	Ditto	2 days	400 km.	$ 20.00
Belém...........	Brasília	Bus	33 hours	2,200 km.	$ 40.00
Brasília.........	Rio de Janeiro	Bus	21 hours	1,000 km.	$ 25.00
			6 weeks	8,002 km.	$219.00 U.S.

and hire canoes.

From Leticia a boat will take you downstream two hours to Benjamin Constant, Brazil, where two-decked boats will carry you to Manaus (five days). The fare includes food. But be warned! Many travelers have become ill, so take your own food. In Manaus, get "stamped in" to Brazil at the downtown police station.

In Manaus, check for boats at *Transnave* (agent for *Enasa* boats), at Rua Marechal Deodoro (Rua means street). Also, try *Agencia Mundiais*, Praca 15 de Novembro,15. 1st Floor (Praca means Plaza).

The river is wide near Manaus all the way to Belém at the mouth of the Amazon. The route is by boat from Manaus to Santarem, then by boat to Santarem to Belém. Buses on a good sealed road run from Belém through Brasilia to Rio de Janeiro. We travelled the Amazon in December, a good time to do so.

At the Zoological Garden in Balém you will find the three-toed sloth. It is a great zoo, with many other attractions, right in the middle of the city.

BIRD-CAGE CARGO BOAT—UCAYALI RIVER, PERU

FACT BOX

Country: Peru, SE

River: Alto Madre de Dios & Madre de Dios

Embarkation Points: Shintuya, Labarinto
  Type of Craft: Motor Canoe
  Time & Distance: 3 Days, 300 km.

Connections:
  Truck: Two days Cuzco—Shintuya, via Patria (250 km.)
    Trucks leave from Ave. T. Panti Pata, near the Puno train station on Monday, Wednesday and Friday.
  Air: Cuzco—Maldonado

Options:

The Manú National Park is almost two days upriver from Boca Manú. A permit is needed to visit the park and can be obtained in Cuzco at the park office in the agriculture department next to the town hall. Allow a week for the Shintuya, Pakitsa, Shintuya trip, and about $200 per person.

No river craft go all the way to Maldonado, but there are good connections for the two hour ride from Labarinto to Maldonado.

Downstream from Maldonado are two jungle lodges: The Explorer's Inn and Cuzco Amazonicas.

> *The following piece, by Hilary, was written about our first trip to Manú in 1973. We have included it here, with a 1980 update, because it accurately describes the frustrations and difficulties of traveling on remote, unfrequented rivers all over South America. Editor.*

This Is Manú

After spending two months in the Andes we needed a change. What we were looking for was our ultimate adventure. We wanted to go further than any road, traveling by river to the village of Manú, then down the Madre de Dios to Puerto Maldonado. From there we knew about buses back to Cuzco.

Just getting to the Alto Madre de Dios river was complicated and uncomfortable. We eventually found a truck going in the right direction and squeezed in with our fellow travelers, mostly coca chewing Indians. Soon we were shivering over a 5,000 m. pass before descending into the lush jungle with butterflies shimmering beside the road. We found a hotel in Patria, and the next day left for Shintuya on a battered timber truck proudly bearing the slogan: Never Late. The doors and hood were missing, but it bounced along while we hung on to our backpacks. The end of the road came suddenly; a bridge had

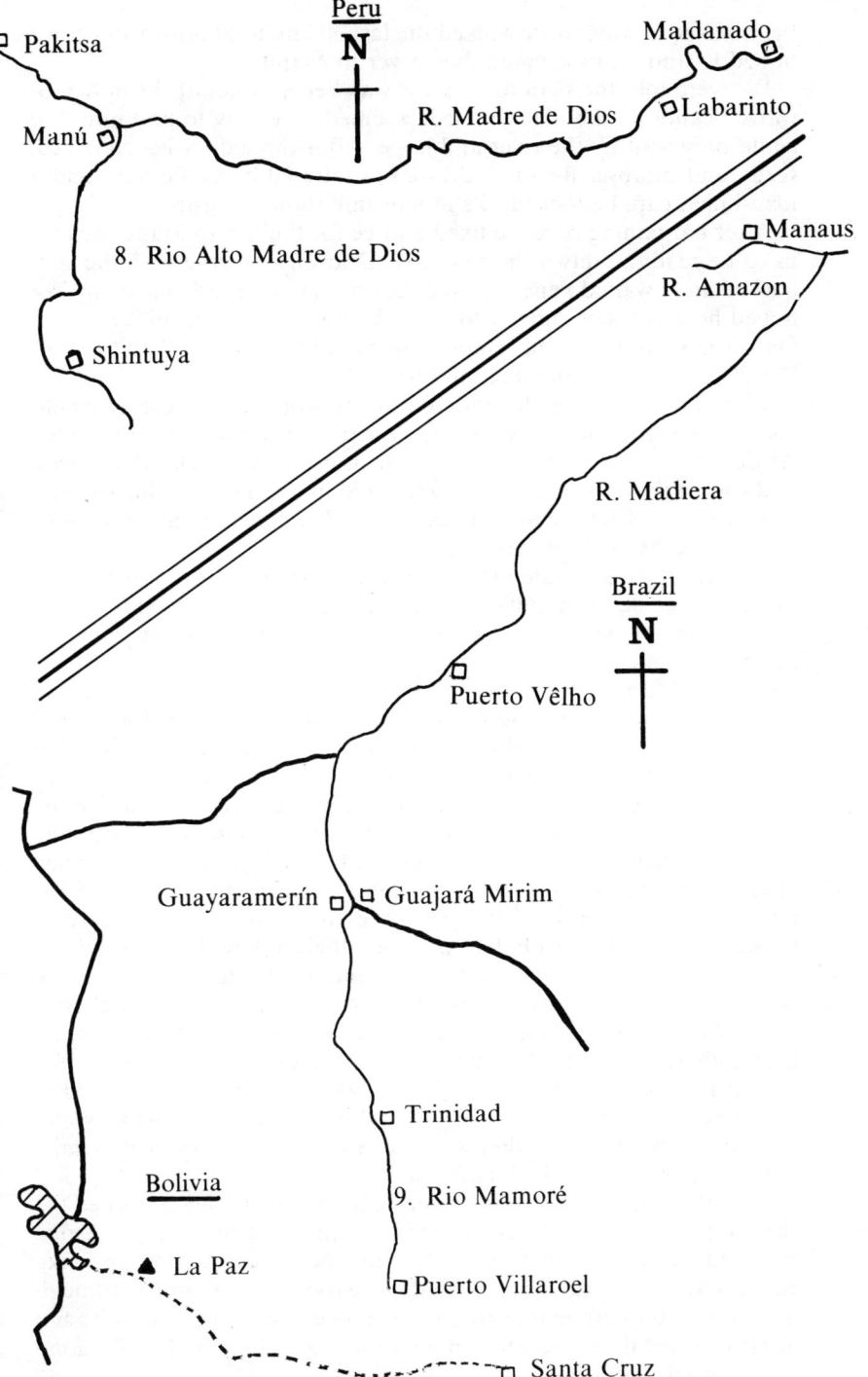

been washed away, so we walked the last 30 km. to Shintuya where we hoped to find a canoe going downriver to Manú.

We were told the man to look for was Pepe, owner of the only motorized canoe in the area. Nobody seemed sure how to find him. We could only wait by the river and hope. After three days Pepe arrived, seedy and morose. Bearded, dressed in tattered battle fatigues and a long-billed cap, he looked like a poor imitation of Castro.

After bargaining hard we fixed a price for the trip to Manú; he told us to be ready at dawn the next day. Dutifully we rose with the sun, packed and awaited Pepe. At 3 pm. he arrived, red-eyed and mean. We hoped he was sober enough to steer the boat down this difficult river. Our progress was indeed erratic, due more to low water than to Pepe. We often got out of the boat and walked.

With our slow progress and late start we wondered where we would spend the night; clearly we wouldn't arrive in Manú until tomorrow. At dusk we turned off the main river into a clear, backwater stream and soon a small cluster of huts appeared in a jungle clearing. After a fine supper of wild pig and yucca we bedded down in one of the huts surrounded by snoring men.

We set off in good time the following morning and in a few hours came to four deserted huts. Pepe pulled in toward the bank. "This is where you get out," he said. "But we are going to Manú," we explained.

"This *is* Manú."

We must have looked so aghast that even Pepe softened a bit and agreed to take us across the river where we found an oil exploration camp. They should be able to help us. The man in charge seemed delighted to have visitors and immediately invited us to lunch. He listened to our plans with interest, but was discouraging about the chances of getting a boat to Maldonado. He explained that the stretch of river we wanted to travel was made dangerous by tricky currents, fallen trees and "Indios." We remembered the stories we'd heard of the savage Machagenga Indian tribe and their link with the disappearance of explorers in the past. We wanted adventure, yes, but we wanted to come out alive! And yet to go back the way we had come seemed such defeat. Then our friend said, "Of course if you don't mind flying, there's a plane leaving for Maldonado this afternoon." We should have known this sounded too good to be true; when it didn't arrive he invited us to stay until the following day. The plane would certainly come if the weather was fine. Since it was carrying dynamite it was important that the landing strip was dry.

We stayed in that camp for five days. It was not unpleasant when the sun came out. We explored paths in the jungle where we saw exotic birds and insects, and once nearly stepped on an enormous snake coiled across our path. There was also the river for swimming although it took a certain amount of courage, not because of the crocodiles but because a female appearance in a swimming suit in an all male camp did not pass unnoticed.

Each day nobody knew whether the plane would land or not, and it was never so wet that we could safely abandon hope nor so dry that we could be sure that it would come. It was a frustrating time. On the fifth day, when the weather was hot and sunny the bombshell came. A man from the camp came to our tent and said, "You must pack immediately. Pepe's here. Since he brought you, he must take you away." We asked about the plane but he simply shook his head and said, "You must go with Pepe."

We had become obsessional in our desire to get to Puerto Maldonado. Our plans, after all this waiting, were a disaster. Pepe, in his usual state of inebriation, looked as morose as we did. Together we set off downriver. Funny, surely that was the wrong direction? He went about a kilometer, then stopped at a jungle hut. "I've got a headache," he said, "we'll start tomorrow." We pleaded with him to at least take us back to the camp; we gave him half our medicine supplies, we cajoled, we humored him, but to no avail.

He dumped our luggage on the bank and chugged away. Just as he was drawing out of sight we heard the sound we'd been waiting for. A light plane was landing across the river at the camp. Frantically we looked downriver. No Pepe. "Have you got a canoe?" we shouted at the hut's owner. He hadn't and there were no other huts nearby, no canoes anywhere. We stood silently. After a while we saw the plane rise over the jungle and set its course for Puerto Maldonado. I sat down and cried as George set up the tent.

Manu Update

In 1980 I was asked to lead the Peru Jungle Expedition for South American Wilderness Adventures. When told our route would include the Alto Madre de Dios, the Manú National Park and Puerto Maldonado I eagerly accepted the offer. I wanted to find out whether the trip we had first attempted was indeed possible, and to see whatever changes had happened.

The trip from Shintuya, via Manú, to Puerto Labarinto (upstream from Puerto Maldonado) is certainly possible. Since gold has been discovered at about the halfway point there is more river traffic. And the jungle has reclaimed both the oil camp and the airstrip, and perhaps even Pepe as he was nowhere to be found.

Since our earlier visit the Manú National Park has been formed, encompassing about 14,000 km^2. and should be visited if at all possible. The headquarters of the park are located at Pakitsa, 15 hours upstream from Boca Manú.

At Pakitsa you will find a shelf of bottles and skulls (the museum), and a football field for pitching your tent. Despite the various trails around the headquarters you will see more animals and birds along the river between Manú and Pakitsa and beyond.

Spider, woolly, howler, and black-capped capuchin monkeys are frequently seen. Early one morning a jaguar was sited on the riverbank below Pakitsa. We saw six river otters resting on the bank above the river, capybara, and at least 200 bird species. Crocs and turtles basked on the beaches and logs. It was a great trip.

PEKE–PEKE ENGINE, PHOTO: G. BRADT

FACT BOX

Country: Bolivia

River: Alto Mamoré

Embarkation Points: Puerto Villaroel, Trinidad
  Types of Craft: Cargo Boats
  Classes & Cost: Hammock $25
  Time & Distance: 5 Days, 400 km.

Connections:
  Bus: Cochabamba—Puerto Villaroel 250 km. 6 hours
  Air: La Paz—Trinidad   Trinidad—La Paz

Options:
  Eight to ten days further downriver, about 700 km., is Guayaramerín (Small Pebble), Bolivia. Across the river: Guajará Mirim, Brazil. From here it is possible to go 400 km. by bus, by-passing rapids, to Puerto Vêlho. From Puerto Vêlho it is 10 days, about $40, and 1,000 km. to Manaus.

Alto Mamoré

Puerto Villaroel to Trinidad on the Rio Mamoré.

Just two days after leaving La Paz we were at Puerto Villaroel, straight east from the capital, on the Rio Ichilo. We had heard of the five day trip to Trinidad, but didn't know if it was still possible. We were fortunate in finding a good looking boat, the *Moby Dick,* loaded and about to leave for Trinidad with a cargo of gravel. The captain was agreeable, set a reasonable price and suggested we buy supplemental supplies in case we didn't like the cooking on board.

    Once on the river we realized how lucky we were to be making the trip. It was a narrow river, teaming with birds such as storks and herons. Toward sunset that first afternoon six magnificent blue and yellow macaws flew across the river ahead of us. They were followed by four red and blue macaws, and next a toucan. A small crocodile loped down to the water's edge and plunged in. We hated to see the day end, but inevitably the sun set. We were slightly anxious about supper because of the captain's warning, but we needn't have been.

    Who, after all, would scorn turtle meat? Real turtle. Had we not known what it was, we would have identified it as pork, so subtle was its flavor. Only the legs are eaten, the innards discarded. Even with three turtles in reserve the captain never missed an opportunity to go ashore to buy freshly jerked *chancho de monte,* or peccary.

    Our first full day on board was much like the next four. The pilot and engineer got up at the first light, started the engine and cast off. Our noisy two cylinder diesel engine woke everyone else up shortly thereafter. We then cruised downriver through the low, purple mists, close to the water. Not long afterward the sun, a huge Chinese-red disk, moved up through the still dark greenery.

As the light became stronger the cook brought hot, sweet, black coffee. Breakfast at 8 usually included a boiled mash of bananas, corn, onions and any supper leftovers. Spiced with pickled red-hot peppers one can happily eat platefuls of this stuff. After breakfast we climbed onto one of the gravel barges and dangled our feet in the water, watching the birds.

After they disappear into their cool bowers, we read until lunch. It was the main meal of the day and usually consisted of a meat dish, two heavy starches, soup and perhaps a vegetable or two. It warranted a *siesta*. During the day we slept in our hammocks in the diningroom where it was breezy and shaded.

Upon waking, more reading, foot dangling and looking for capybara (*ronsoco*), the world's largest rodent. Being unwearable and inedible this mammal has no fear of man nor engines. We saw a herd of fifteen, but seeing a hundred animals in a group isn't unusual.

At about 4 pm. the birds began to reappear in large numbers. Many were feeding, swooping low over the river, or diving through the air high above. Parrots screeched in flocks, on their way home to their nests in hollow trees, scores of other birds took wing as we passed. The pilot began searching the banks for a suitable haven for the night. When he found deep water beside a steep bank we turned upstream and glided toward the cliff. A crewman scrambled up the bank with a rope which he tied around a clump of trees.

After a skimpy supper (compared to breakfast and lunch) the crew played various board and card games and turned in early. By 9 pm. everything was quiet on board. We pitched our tent on the foredeck, crawled inside and listened to the jungle, the water sliding by, fish jumping and mosquitoes whining.

CAPYBARA

Huevos

By George Bradt

We were traveling down a narrow river, the Upper Mamoré in Bolivia. Behind us lay the Andes and the Altiplano, while ahead were the Madiera and eventually the Amazon. Our boat, the *Moby Dick*, was bound for Port Trinidad five days downstream with a cargo of gravel. Suddenly, as we sat dangling our legs in the cool water, great excitement broke out on every quarter. The *Moby Dick* ponderously turned upstream, treading the water just enough to remain stationary against the brown current. At the first shouts most of the crew jumped into the long, tippy dugout and were soon out of the craft onto the opposite shore. The canoe was paddled back for us and the captain. Once ashore he pointed to tracks leading from the water's edge toward high, dry sand and then back to the water. Apparently the crew had spotted these tracks from the boat.

More tracks were visible now that we knew what to look for. But why the hysteria? "Huevos," said the captain. Of course: turtle eggs! Each set of parallel tracks led to a next in the warm sand. Now we noticed a freshly dug hole at the end of each track, but no one knew if the nests yielded eggs, since crew-members from another boat had preceded us. Eventually we found more tracks which the others had missed in their excitement, digging deep down into the slightly damp sand we found an egg. Many more were scattered deeper throughout the warm sand, nearly twenty in all. We handled them gently, although the captain illustrated their invincibility by dropping one from his shoulder; it simply bounced. Their white shells were indeed rubbery, squashy and the size of a ping-pong ball.

When the captain thought we had exhausted our search, back we went to the canoe and were paddled out to the *Moby Dick*, still patiently battling the current. After three steamy blasts from the boat's whistle the opposite beach was again filled with crew-members. Once on board we saw their incredibly bountiful haul: they had collected dozens and dozens of eggs.

Shortly after the boat resumed its course a plateful of cooked eggs was brought to us. Several crew-members eagerly demonstrated the art of turtle egg eating, then stood around to watch our reaction. Copying their technique, I peeled off half the shell.

The white was still liquid, but I gave the shell a slight squeeze and popped everything neatly into my mouth. A few sceptical chews assured me that I liked turtle eggs. The yolk was dry and slightly granular, but when eaten with the moist white, the taste combined a subtle texture of nuts and butter.

The day after arriving in Trinidad we set off to explore the surrounding area. The earth was ocher, the palms lanky-lean and the undergrowth prolific. We were hoping to see our first rheas (cousins of the ostrich) which range all over southern South America. Darwin encountered thousands.

Today they're still plentiful but difficult to see for two reasons: firstly they've retreated into remote areas, and secondly their natural coloring blends perfectly with their surroundings. We saw none, but encountered an old man sitting beside the road with a sack of perfectly oval, huge creamy white eggs. Eggs, he maintained them to be, but we found it hard to believe. Whose eggs could they be? *Tyrannosaurus rex*? He drew a sketch in the sand. The light dawned. We remembered the ostrich family produces the largest eggs in the world. For fifty cents, one was ours.

Since we had set off from Trinidad without having had breakfast we decided to eat this noble egg as soon as we found someone to cook it for us. Off the main road we saw a small village and eventually located a disheveled restaurant. No sooner had our hostess suggested rhea egg scrambled with onions and peppers than off she went to cook it. We watched her. With one expert crack with a machete, the shell broke into two halves. In a matter of minutes, our plates arrived heaped high with scrambled egg. It was delicious.

RHEA

Scale Chart

MAP SCALE	1" REPRESENTS	1 CM REPRESENTS	1 MILE IS REPRESENTED BY	1 KILOMETER IS REPRESENTED BY
1:63,360	1 mile	.634 km	1 inch	1.58 cm
1:75,000	1.18 mile	.75 km	.845 inch	1.33 cm
1:100,000	1.58 mile	1.0 km	.634 inch	1.0 cm
1:250,000	3.95 mile	2.5 km	.253 inch	4.0 mm
1:500,000	7.89 mile	5.0 km	.127 inch	2.0 mm
1:1,000,000	15.78 mile	10.0 km	.063 inch	1.0 mm
1:1,500,000	23.67 mile	15.0 km	.042 inch	.666 mm

The left side of the table is labeled LARGER SCALES (top rows) and SMALLER SCALES (bottom rows).

INCA FLOATS

5982 Balboa Drive, Oakland, CA-94611
Tel. (415) 339-9095
South & Central American Expeditions.
Horse Treks, float trips, photography and
natural history excursions.

SUBSCRIBE to EXPEDITION

Expedition is the first magazine of its kind: written, edited, printed and mailed while enroute throughout the Americas. How well it succeeds is entirely up to you. We need support through subscriptions and reader interest. Each issue of **Expedition** is filled with adventure, facts, insights, and features as diverse as latin culture, archaeology and marine life.

Get a copy, we are worth discovering as we discover the Americas.

Annual subscription

U.S. 11.00
Canada 15.00
Mexico 235 P
Belize 22.00BH

Panama BII.00
Japan 16.00
England 16.00
Europe 16.00

720-36th Avenue North
St. Petersburg, Florida
33704 U.S.A.

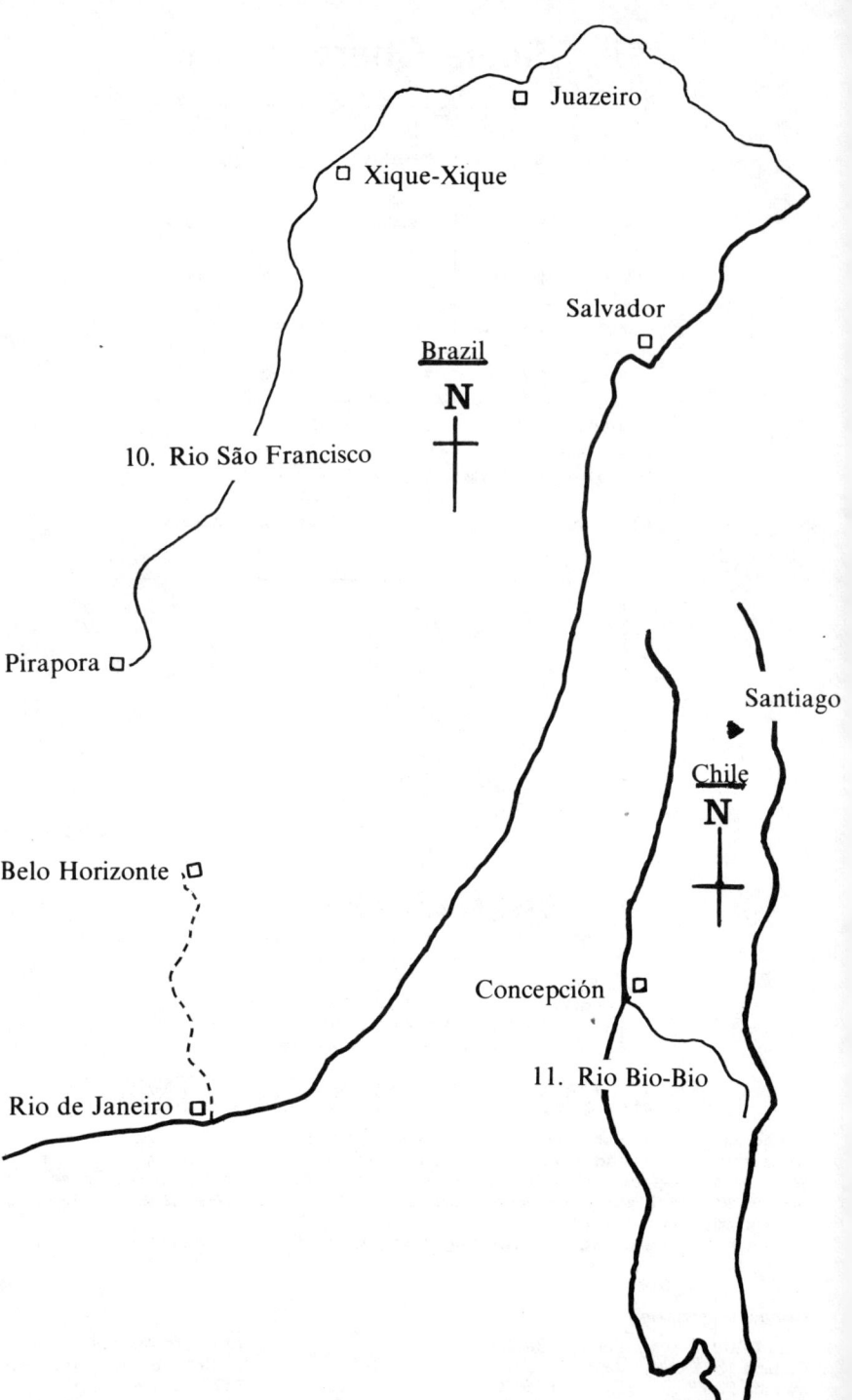

South of the Amazon Basin

FACT BOX

Country: Brazil, SE
River: São Francisco
Embarkation Points: Pirapora, Bom Jesus, Xique Xique, Juazeiro
  Type of Craft: Large Cargo Boats
  Classes & Costs: Double Cabin with Bath: $225 per person
                    Double Cabin without Bath: $185 per person
                    Hammock: $30 per person
  Time & Distance: 7 Days, 1,300 km.
  Schedule: Lv. Pirapora on 10th and 25th
            Lv. Juazeiro on 3rd and 18th
  Address: Companhia de Navegação do São Francisco (CNSF)
           Ave. São Francisco 1363, Pirapora, Minas Gerais
                                  or
           Rua Coronel Aprigio Duarte 3, Juazeiro, Bahia
Connections:
  Bus: Belo Horizonte to Pirapora; Juazeiro to Recife
  Rail: Rio de Janeiro to Pirapora; Juazeiro to Salvador
Options:
  Visit Brasília, Brasília National Park (no permit needed)

Rio São Francisco
By Nick Ryalls

After a delicious breakfast in Pirapora we marched to our boat. And what a boat! Like something off the Mississippi. A showboat, the *São Francisco*, a real ugly beauty powered by steam, with logs piled high in the bows and lower decks. We traveled first class, a cabin with hot water. At 10 am. (only half an hour late) we set off, watched by most of the youth of the town. What else ever happens in Pirapora?

Seeing the settlements on the riverbanks make real the pervasize poverty of Brazil; not just the absence of money, but the poverty of day-to-day life. Strange that with so much open space people prefer to cluster in cells like Rio de Janeiro or São Paulo. Yet not so strange perhaps. Who could cope with a country as vast as Brazil?

The Rio São Francisco is wide, about 500 m. across. We traveled downstream, north. It was so peaceful, restful. The riverboat seems to breathe, like a living thing, quietly, not at all like a machine.

Dinner call! We missed seeing the sun set, yes, but having dinner we witnessed one of the most magically beautiful sights in the world: the slow departure of light, the withdrawal of day from this side of the world. Picture postcards show it, and we scoff, "No, that's too much, they've overdone those colors." But the real thing was dazzling; the merging of red, orange, lilac, violet, purple and crimson until the blackness covers all except the moon, shining like a silver fingernail clipping. Above it the pole-star burned with piercing, brilliant, diamond light, totally upstaging all the lesser stars. Darkness surrounded the boat completely. Lights appear from the bank from time to time, flicker, as if they were candles. We leave them behind as we move steadily on; their reflections shimmer on the surface of the water as in a liquid mirror.

Music from the lower decks—a drum, a tambourine, a pipewhistle, and voices. We could be in Africa, the sound is so African. Another boat passed giving us some idea of our own reflection. The boat looked beautiful as it broke the darkness, leaving gold and silver mirrored streaks. After it's gone only the darkness remains.

Although only first day, we've eaten better than we expected: rice and black beans were on the menu, and pasta, cabbage, tomatoes, peppers. Beef too, but that was for lunch. Tonight we had fish, which was pleasant, caught from the river. After supper we still felt a little hungry, surprising after the amount we ate. Tiredness overcame us although only 7:45 pm. No mosquitoes, although a few moths fluttered around the fluorescent lights.

We stopped for twenty minutes to stock up on wood. An amazing, intriguing sight: four men wore only blue cotton shorts, and white vests, with a piece of sacking covering their heads like a hood and extending to their ankles, load the wood. They carried hefty loads already cut into metered lengths and stacked near the steeply sloping riverbank. When the new wood was stoked into the furnaces it sent red glowing sparks sprouting from the funnel, dancing like flying glow worms into the water.

At dawn the boat stopped at the town of São Francisco, 234 km. downstream from Pirapora. People came down the stone quay to watch us. A standing man and boy paddled their dugout, large market tents billowed along the riverbank and a colonial style church loomed over the trees and town. The houses looked dreary though painted blue, green, yellow, and strawberry-pink.

After breakfasting on bread, sweet rolls, coffee and a delicious papaya we went to sit in the bow of the boat. In front of us the ship's bell inscribed: Steamboat Olinda 1912. The river was muddy, but not wide. The boat can not take a course straight down the river, but zig-zags following the deep-water channel.

The land is completely flat though yesterday we saw a solitary clump of loaf-shaped mountains, brownish-purple in the distance. Today nothing breaks the horizon except trees. Nothing to see except almost 180° of blue, blue sky; 178° of river and 1° of land on either bank.

The concept of time must be quite different for people here. Time must pass quickly for them, as there is so little to fill it with. Time just passes. Light defines time here, not some horrible alarm clock or office timetable.

The boat has stopped a Januaria, renowned for its production of the fiery sugarcane rum. The label on the bottle reads: "Aguardente" which maybe translates as burning water, or water for your teeth. Little more can be said of the place except for a dusty main street supporting a few shops, a modern church with stained glass, and a public library.

We met women washing in the river. The bushes around them were hung with clothes drying in the sun. We chatted and found they lived in a village 8 km. away. They carried their bowls of washing on their heads here every day because this is the nearest water; they came a second time to fetch water for cooking and drinking. As we went further along the dusty track, we encountered a cart drawn by fearsome looking oxen laden with rice, beans, and dried fish.

Another magical nightfall.

We've landed, after many bumps against sandbars in the night, at Bom Jesus de Lapa. We got up to have a look but there was little to see except some local folk and the town taxi. The town is famous for its church built into the side of a massive rock. The mountain is the only protuberance above the horizon. This morning's breakfast included *minga*, a sweet, creamy porridge with cinnamon sprinkled on top.

An afternoon stop allowed swimmers to have a splash; the captain got angry when everyone didn't come on board when he tooted. We started moving off with one of our passengers left on shore. He couldn't swim, but walked confidently into the water holding his expensive camera and zoom lens above his head. The water got higher and higher, nearly up to his nose, when a passing dugout gave him a lift back to the boat. What a fate to be marooned in the middle of nowhere with only a camera and a bathing suit.

We went ashore on the last night. The huts on the mud-flats were made of twigs and branches interwoven with bits of cardboard. Heaven help the occupants when it rained. Their huts doubled as market stalls where bits of dried fish, bread and coffee were sold. Even with small oil lamps the shacks were dark and gloomy.

We stopped at Barra for more wood, cedar this time. We found a beautiful white church looking onto a large quiet square. Dinner arrived, a red side of beef drawn in a horse cart.

Two little girls came on board to sell oranges. The eldest was twelve, but looked much younger and smaller. We talked to them and found they had made a four day journey on foot, alone, to get the oranges, then a three day trip to the boat. They could not read or count. Their village had a school, but the only teacher left four years ago. Some of the boys we talked to couldn't read either, but they knew the flags of the famous football teams from Rio and São Paulo.

After a blast on the ship's hooter, sounding like a giant blowing across the top of a bottle, we were off again downstream. We seem to be hitting sandbanks more often now. Last night the boat anchored rather than attempting a treacherous part of the river in darkness. We reached Sobrado (Sobradinho) just after our last lunch of cold spaghetti, beef and the ever faithful rice and beans.

From here we went to Juazeiro by car, then on to Petrolina and the bus to Recife. Petrolina's Hotel Grande do Rio really was grand. Beautiful rooms, leather chairs and elegant furniture. Dinner that evening was spectacular: fresh vegetables, hot bread, heart of palm salad, and a ham and cheese omelette with french fries on the side. We could barely haul ourselves to our room and sleep.

Delicious fresh fruit and lots of coffee got us started the next morning. We purchased our bus tickets for the twelve hour, 780 km. trip to Recife, across the entire state of Pernambuco.

> *Pyrethrum is a plant* (Chrysanthemum genus) *used as an insecticide. Throughout the Amazon basin you will find fragile coils of pyrethrum sold in many of the general stores. The coils, usually made in the east, are burned like incense and are effective against mosquitos in a room at night. One coil usually lasts six to eight hours. The metal stand, with a prong, is used to hold the coil off any surfaces which might burn.*

Excursions   With the possible exceptions of Manaus and Iquitos we doubt there are any towns in the entire Amazon basin capable of entertaining a visitor for more than a day. That's fine if you have only one day, but if you are waiting for a plane or a boat you'll start feeling restless, especially if you are on a tight time schedule.

In these circumstances visitors should make the most of the local area, using the town as a base for explorations outward into the surrounding countryside. There will be roads, buses, taxis, canoes to hire, motor boats and often there are local water taxis to the opposite shore. Some of our most memorable river trips were exciting because we arrived unexpectedly in a new and different place to explore.

Chatting with the hotel staff, visiting the local tourist office or asking the nearest travel agent are good ways of finding out what is happening in an area. The local school will have someone who knows the area and will speak English. The Port Captain will undoubtedly have a few ideas as well.

There is no excuse to be in a new place, locked in your hotel room, waiting for something to happen. After all, if you are adventurous enough to have gotten this far, why not go a little further?

FACT BOX

Country: Chile
River: Bio-Bio
Embarkation Points: Lake Galletue 25 km. E. of Volcan Llaima
  Type of Craft: Rubber Raft
  Classes & Costs: Travel with SOBEK, listed under service organizations
  Time & Distance: 7 Days, 150 km.
Season: December, January, February
Options:
  There is no way to do this trip unless you go as part of a fully organized and equipped expedition.

Rio Bio-Bio

By Richard Bangs

It was a long shot: we knew nothing about the Bio-Bio except that it is Chile's second longest river. We had no hydrological data, no flow charts, not even good maps; for all we knew the eddies south of the equator spun counter-clockwise. If we had been asked to rank the ten least likely countries of the world where one would find runnable rafting rivers, Chile would have been close to the top.

The Bio-Bio, an onomatopoetic Mapuche Indian word for the song of a local bird, rises from Lago Galletue, a shimmering alpine lake backdropped by Volcan Llaima and just a few kilometers west of the Argentine border. The river flows in a grand arc which skews south then heads west, passing through the villages of Santa Barbara and Los Angeles before spilling into the Pacific at Concepción.

Seven of us finally congregated at the San Francisco airport; Stan, perhaps the most sensible, got cold feet at the ticket counter and decided to go skiing instead. As he was swallowed by the crowd we wondered if his wasn't the best choice. Had he a vision? A psychic premonition? Would the river be too rough? The plane crash? It was Friday the 13th.

In no time we were beside the Bio-Bio near the lake. Local residents kill a lamb for us, cut its throat, collected the hot blood in a wooden bowl, drop in a lemon wedge coagulating the blood into chunks like four-day-old cafeteria Jello and offer us *Nachi,* a delicacy, kept for special occasions.

A condor catches an air current overhead as we shove our two inflatable rafts into the water. We spin into the current and whirl downstream. The first rapids are shallow, rocky, couched in a small canyon topped with spidery Araucania (*Araucaria*) trees. These eerie pines, often called Monkey Puzzle trees, cast a magical aura over the river. Twisting through this water maze we are struck with a ghostly feeling of unreality; the river is like none other we've ever experienced.

The River Styx might bear some semblance or the Forest River in Middle-earth. Stands of spindle-shanked Monkey Puzzle trees hover over us like the arms and fingers of a vast demon.

The water is crisp, clear as *pisco*; it almost crackles with each stroke. As we pump and flail through channels and chutes we drink in the scenery. The area we are traversing is called the 'Switzerland of South America' but that does not give it justice. Switzerland should be called the 'Bio-Bio of Europe.' The snow-capped Andes, an endless phalanx of two dimensional points blend with sky and clouds. Closer, in royal symmetry, stands the perfect, snow-dipped cone of Volcan Llaima, an indifferent sentry watching us scurry like stirred ants.

For the first 40 km. the river twists on a broad foothill-plateau, level fields extending to the bases of the mountains. The landscape is smooth and sweet, as are the rapids. *Caballeros*, decked in leather, gape down at the *gringos locos* swirling beneath them. Horses, pigs and sheep wander the fields above cobbled banks; banks that look like a Renaissance road turned on its side.

We float among black-faced ibis, black cormorants, Chiloe widgeons, torrent ducks and two types of seagull. There are hundreds of Magellan geese, slow moving and dim-witted.

We camp on a long, green velour embankment with a vista of saw-toothed, snow-draped peaks. Our first night: fresh vegetables and fruit under a crisp sky speckled with unfamiliar stars for entertainment.

As we lose elevation the flora and geology begin changing. We wind through groves of cedar, Lombardy poplar and cyprus festooned with long shags of Spanish moss. Beneath the trees, spread like a rumpled blanket, are fields of mullin, single-stalked plants erupting with yellow blossoms. The river begins slicing through a layer of basalt, falling into a burnished gorge. Evidence of people begins to disappear. There's a sense of sliding into oblivion, leaving behind the commonplace. But at a creek we pass a lone fisherman working a line with a crude sapling pole. This prompts Bill to try his luck. He casts, and seconds later a strike. A two kg. German brown trout flops into the bilge. He lands another. Bill is in eighth heaven.

We purl past the last semblance of civilization for the next 175 km: Chilpaca, a ghost town that had thrived during the gold strike of 1932. We fade into a forested vortex as the sun drops past a distant volcano. Camp is at a tributary: a pure white cascade, tremendous and frothing.

It is Saturday morning, the weekend, so we treat it as such; kick back and soak in some time. Scanning through the maps we pinpoint our location; there's a lake up the tributary five km, so we investigate. It's there, and it's beautiful. Lago Jesus Maria is deep blue, sun-dappled and trapped in a glacial cirque. Reflected in the surface are the 3,000 m. granite points, spires and flutes, with tears of snow running down steep combs. It could be one of the Twin Lakes at Yosemite, only no backpackers and 25,000 km. south.

By noon we're running downstream again, splashing and careening through scores of rapids: "Pelegroso Plunge," "Bangs Bane," "Morrison Falls." The river seems a combination of many of the best rivers stateside, powerful scenery, powerful rapids, clear water, good fishing. The afternoon brings bigger rapids still, and more new names: "Luisita's Score," after a 1952 paperback porno book, and "Boor's Paradise," after Stan Boor, the man who left the trip at the airport.

We pull over to a tributary, the Rio Lloco, and discover mineral hot springs. "Doesn't this river ever stop? What more can it give us?" Someone complains. But the river doesn't hear. After a soothing soak, we head downstream and hit the first of the really big rapids. Suddenly we're in water so violent and complex it sends pulses and spirits soaring. One rapid has a glacier-shaped glassy chute, a four meter drop, then stops in a back-rolling column of water looking like a horizontal tornado. Next a 500 m. labyrinth, through a team of basalt gridirons positioned like the Bears defensive line. In the middle of this rock-maze a glacial stream, gray with flour, spits into the river. As we scramble up the bank to scout we can see the source of the stream, a fantastic glint of ice pouring down a mammoth mountain cleft. The brilliant, blue glacier carves through black basalt and ash. As we climb higher the view gets more spectacular. The glacier is a mere ornament hanging from the 6,000 m. cone of active Volcan Callaqui. Its belching, smoking, snowy peak looms over the river. After soaking in this scene we turn our attentions to the river, and the rapid.

It takes us 25 minutes to memorize the run, zig-zagging through rocks like a pinball on the Captain Fantastic machine. We begin the run, pumping the oars wildly and trying to match the map in my mind with the frothy reality crashing down the bow. The current is so torrential, the perspective so different, we lose our way. We stroke like crazy, but can't tell where we're going. We pull hard to miss an approaching linebacker and suddenly realize we won't make it. Whack! The boat buckles, rebounds, fibrilates then snaps around the wrong side of the rock, straight toward a deep hole. Miraculously we're all still in the boat; we brace for the hole. It swallows us, fills us with enzymes, digests us and poops us out whole, like corn on a camping trip. We made it. We can't believe it. Before blood vessels can relax, the view downstream sets all hearts into overdrive. Just 200 m. below, one of the most incredible sights: a 45 m. tributary waterfall leaps in shimmering light. It reflects off a sheer basalt cliff and describes a gentle arc as it crashes into the river. It's impossible to imagine such a display of water and light falling and mixing directly into the main river.

To continue past this remarkable sight would be a crime of the first order; we pull in across from the falls, and make camp on a boulder pile. Certainly there are more comfortable campsites nearby, but the view from here couldn't be matched by a thousand Posturpedic nights.

Just after sunrise we march down to the river and scout the rapid. It's the biggest yet; a fuming, mad jitterbug of water dancing through king-size holes and bouncing off immense boulders. Past all this there are 500 m. of fast water. Then the river pinches against the south wall creating a toboggan run through six major souse-holes and twice as

BIO-BIO RIVER, CHILE, PHOTO: R. BANGS

many tidal waves. Finally, there is a long, sleepy stretch of water where men, boats and pieces could be picked up, should we decide to run this one. Climbing out of this canyon to make a one km. portage over slippery terrain didn't seem realistic, so we decide to run it, though the consequences of a mistake could be dear. Bruce rows first, with Bill and me riding the bow.

Bruce makes a good entry but smacks a lateral wave which turns him the wrong way. We're washed broadside against a small mountain bisecting the river; the boat rides up on its side, the first stage of a flip. Bill and I throw our weight on the rising tube and the boat slides off the rock, round the far side and into a channel. We're out of control in unknown water, on the defensive now. We careen off a pair of basalt pinnacle slabs, smash an oar, spin on our side and flop down to the rapid's end, rightside up but full of water. We bail frantically as Bruce pulls toward shore. We made it.

At another sharp rapid Jack and George are kicked out of the boat. Jack somehow ends up dangling helplessly upside down in the water, with his tennis shoe caught on the thoe pin. He struggles to keep his chin above water and wrench his shoe free, while the boat drifts toward the next cataract, a bad one. The scene seems too melodramatic to be real, but a watery scream from Jack cracks any veneer of illusion. George splashes back into the bilge, grabs the oars and wrestles the raft toward shore, while Mike plunges in and pulls the caught leg free. Coughing and sputtering Jack drags himself onto the beach, a vacant, hurt look in his eyes. It had been close.

Bruce pays his dues later in the day. He decides to run left through a rapid Jack had already run to the right; a mistake. Suddenly we're plummeting through space toward a rock at the bottom of a four meter hole. We smack, buckle, twist and almost flip. Bruce hurtles overboard, I spring to the oars just as the raft slams into a cliff. We bounce off and spin into an eddy. No sign of Bruce. Long seconds pass; steel-cold seconds, the worst may have happened. We feel the floor bump twice and a blue Bruce pops up next to the boat, alive and gasping.

The day has been too intense to continue on. We've run more rapids in a single day than are run on twelve days on the Colorado, and most were bigger than the Colorado's biggest.

Tuesday morning, crisp and bell clear we whiz through a stream of thrilling rapids. At noon we reach a red light. The river narrows to barely 20 m. wide and zig-zags through two tortuous right-angle turns. Most of the water jets around the first corner, slides down a three meter sluice and crashes into an overhanging cliff on the right. Overhangs are the real killers; each year they eat a few hapless kayakers and an occasional rafter. If someone falls out of a boat and gets swept into an overhang, hundreds of kilos of water pressure make escape impossible. This, coupled with the fact that the next three rapids, all in close succession, are horrendous, gives us pause for thought and some serious scouting.

"Whatever you do, stay away from that wall, Rich," warned Jack as we pushed off. The melodrama in his voice put a lump in my throat. Now that the wall was bearing down on us at 60 km/h. I could see the dark recesses of the overhang growing more ominous. I jump back just as we hit the wall at a 45° angle and began sliding up the wall. After climbing up and wedging in the overhang, the raft tipped over as we jump clear and are flushed safely down into the eddy. It is Jack's first flip after rafting for ten years!

We continue through the next rapid without mishap (if we hadn't been scared to death it would have been fun) and came to the third big one. We could see the water colliding with a boulder as big as the Ritz, splitting into two channels each spitting, slobbering 5,000 m.^{2} of water per second. It makes Lava Falls look like a cesspool.

We portage. This involves unloading all our gear, lugging it 100 m. up and down little mountains, lining the boats with a lot of pushing and shoving through the rapids. It's difficult to communicate because of the deafening roar. Somehow we get it done and in two hours we're back in the boats, tossing on whitecaps as we lash the duffel down. We scout the fourth rapid, run it easily and camp two km. downstream on the north bank. After a long, tough, satisfying day we raise a few glasses, dine on spaghetti, soup, pudding, then lay back for another starry night with the sound of our crazy, beautiful river just a few meters away.

Wednesday. George spends breakfast examining the maps, and makes a grim announcement. He thinks the contour lines indicate the next stretch of twelve kilometers drops twice as much as yesterday's rapids did, and those were the worst we'd ever seen. An encouraging start to the day.

We push off and run a riffle, but suddenly it turns into a formidable rapid, and this is just our introduction. George smacks every big wave and reversal; we come within centimeters of capsizing and I loose precious hair. Then, without warning, we enter another rapid. This time Jack is swept out of the boat, but is back in quickly. Next, George catapults straight out of the bow. The wildness continues all morning. Despite seven days in the sun everyone's face is wan, knuckles are blue. Then the rapids slowly begin to ease and we notice the canyon walls tapering down. We notice the mountains receding. We realize, with mixed emotions, that we're through and all in one piece.

The wilderness of the world at your fingertips. Whitewater rafting, trekking, sailing, mountaineering, scuba diving, skiing, wildlife viewing, art and cultural tours, and general excursions to the most remote corners of the globe. We cover six continents, twelve months a year. The finest in experienced and knowledgeable guides, small groups, fine food, personal attention to each client's needs before, during and after the trip, and an imaginative and aggressive program keeping Sobek in the vanguard of adventure travel all guarantee the experience of a lifetime.

Appendices

U.S. & Metric Equivalents

Conversion formulae:

5,280 feet = 1 mile = 1,609.344 meters exactly

1 mile = 1.6 km   1/4 mile = 400 m.   1 km = 5/8 mile

Kilometers	Miles	Miles	Kilometers
20	12.5	20	32
30	18.5	30	48
40	25	40	64
50	31	50	80.5
60	37	60	96.5
70	43.5	70	113
80	49.5	80	129
90	56	90	145
100	62	100	161

Temperature conversion between Fahrenheit (°F) and Celsius (°C)

$°F = 9/5\,(°C) + 32°$ or $°C = 5/9\,(°F - 32°)$

°F	°C	°F	°C
−40	−40	77	25
0	−18	98.6	37
32	0	104	40
68	20	212	100

1″ = 22 millimeters
1″ = 2.2 centimeters
36″ = .9144 meter
39.37″ = 1 meter
1 knot = 1 nautical mile per hour (Spanish: *Nudo*)
1 nautical mile (6,076′) = 1,852 meters
1 fathom (6′) = 1.83 meters (Spanish: *Braza*)

Dictionary

This list contains only Spanish & Portuguese words of great importance to river travel. We have checked the meaning and spelling with two different sources to come up with words widely used and understood. There are thirty-one distinct languages spoken in the Amazon basin, and in the Shulmatoff book you will find thirty-one different words to describe the same thing. Spanish is widely understood, even by Portuguese speakers, as a root language. Apologize first, then speak Spanish in Brazil; this works fine although you won't be able to understand the answers until your ear gets used to the intonation.

There are no complete phrases here; if you are going to run a river on your own you'd better not need a phrase book. Several years ago two men were killed on the Urabamba, just below Machu-Picchu, because they didn't understand Spanish.

Spanish

Balsa	Synonymous with raft, usually made of Balsa wood (*Ochroma lagopus* or *pyramidale*)
Barbasco	Fish poison collected from a plant
Batelao	Long, wide boat commonly poled
Boga	Paddler
Braza	Fathom, or 1.85 m.
Canoa	Canoe
Cascada	Waterfall
Cataracta	Waterfall
Cebiche	Peru's national fish dish
Chicha	Beer made from any number of ingredients
Cienaga	Swamp
Chinchorro	Hammock (Venezuela & Colombia)
Embarcacion	Boat or Ship
Encuentro	Where two rivers join
Ganaderia	Cattle ranch
Hamaca	Hammock
Invierno	Rainy season
Llanos	Broad, grassy plains in E. Colombia & S. Venezuela
Nudo	1 knot—nautical measure
Peke Peke	16 hp. motor commonly used on highland rivers
Peligro	Danger
Peligroso	Dangerous
Pescado	Fish
Picante	Hot & spicy sauce
Planudo	Flat bottomed boat
Pongo	Deep river gorge, always filled with rapids, marking the limit of the mountain rivers flowing down into the jungle. Peligroso.

Quebrada	Ravine with flowing water in it
Rapidos	Rapids
Red	Net, as in mosquito net
Remolino	Whirlpool
Soga	Rope, especially useful when slinging a hamaca/chinchorro
Verano	Dry season

Portuguese

Caxoeiras	Rapids
Lacustre	Marsh
Piroga	Canoe
Queixadas	Rapids

Good People to Know

Corregidor	High Village official
Jefe de la Marina	Port (Harbor) Captain—Spanish
Capitania do Puerto	Port (Harbor) Captain—Portuguese
Capatian de la Puerto	Port (Harbor) Captain—Spanish

Major Museums, Zoos, Botanical Gardens

Balém   Do Bosque, and Goeldi Museum (Ave. M. Barâta)

Bogotá   Museum of Natural History (Carrera 7 & Calle 26) Archaeological Museum (Carrera 6 No. 7–43)

Lima   Parque de les Leyendas is a fine zoo in a suburb between Lima and Callao.

Maimi   The Fairchild Tropical Gardens, not far from the airport, are an excellent introduction (in English) to tropical and subtropical flora.

Manaus   Museu Indigena (Ave. 7 de Setembro) Botanical Gardens

Rio de Janiero   Meseu do Indio (Rua das Palmeiras 55, Botafogo) In the Quinta Boa Vista park you will find: botanical gardens, the National Museum and the Museum of Hunting & Fishing.

São Paulo   The Butantã Institute is one of the world's foremost snake farms supplying antivenin.

Tingo Maria   Botanical gardens & zoo.

Service Organizations

Amazon Explorers (Manaus) Ltda.   Run various trips from one to several nights in the jungle, with plenty of river travel. They offer a five day trip up the Rio Negro to the Rio Carabinani. Address: Caixa Postal 474, Manaus, Brazil

Amazon River Cruise   Four days by river boat from Iquitos to Leticia. There is also a jungle camp near Iquitos. Address: P.O. Box 39583, Los Angeles, CA 90039   Tel. (800) 423-2791 or (213) 246-4816.

Back Country International   Spend a week on the Apurímac River, after hiking across the Cordillera Vilcabamba. Address: 1804 Magnolia Place, Davis, CA 95616

La Cabana   This jungle lodge near Pucallpa has river boat tours of Amazon tributaries and a small plane for hire. Address: Casilla 43, Pucallpa, Peru

Great Expeditions   Through this organization's bi-monthly newsletter all things are possible: meeting other people interested in river travel and the friendly staff are knowledgeable on a wide variety of travel in South America. Address: P.O. Box 46499, Vancouver, B.C. V6R 4G7, Canada Tel. (604) 738-4222

Inca Floats   This highly qualified group combines river travel with horseback trips through the Andes. Address: 5982 Balboa Drive, Oakland, CA 94611 (415) 339-9095

Jesson Travel   Not only does this travel agency run its own five day balsa raft trips, but it also owns a jungle lodge 12 km. by river from Iquitos. Address: 333 South Flower St. #173, Los Angeles, CA 90071 Tel. (213) 628-2278

Mayac Expediciones   Take a wonderful, whitewater day trip on the Urubamba between Chilca and Pisac. Transportation to and from Cuzco is provided. Address: Procuradores 378 *or:* Apartado 596, Cuzco, Peru

Sobec Expeditions Spend a week rafting the exciting Bio-Bio in Chile with this capable, well organized group. Address: P.O. Box 761, Angels Camp, CA 95222 (209) 736-2661

South American Wilderness Adventures No other outfitter does as many river trips, and more are being added annually. Here is a selection of current offerings:
  Shamans & Healers of Ecuador
  Canoe the Headwaters of the Amazon
  Peru Jungle Expedition (Madre de Dios & Manú National Park)
Address: 1760 Solano Ave., Berkeley, CA 94707 Tel. (415) 524-5111

Tawa Bolivia's jungle is the locale for this group's two week survival course. The ability to speak French would be an asset on this trip. Address: Calle R. Gutierrez 521, *or:* Casilla 8662, La Paz, Bolivia

Tambo Treks Combine a two week backpacking trip with a week of rafting on the Urubamba to the Pongo de Mainique, an impressive gorge. Address: Vicki Weeks, 5210 12th NE, Seattle, WA 98105 Tel. (206) 522-1098

Transcontinental Explore the Amazon basin by kayak or raft (wood or rubber) with this Lima based group. Address: Fred Allert, Jr. Ocoña 180 #408, Tel.: 283995 or 273901

Whitewater

The upper reaches of many South American rivers have not been explored, and few have been run in any sort of craft. While this challenge may not appeal to all our readers, it may come as exciting news to those intrepid souls possessing sound whitewater skills. The South American Explorers Club in Lima will provide more details and information to members, and their excellent quarterly magazine often runs news and articles covering whitewater exploration.

All the rivers listed below are considered Class IV by the International Water Classification which is summarized thus: Rapids, very difficult and dangerous.

Bolivia

Beni, Grande, Pilcomayo.

Colombia

Magdalena, Cauca, Sogamoso

Peru

Apurímac, Marañon, Mantaro, Urubamba, Huallaga, Pampa, Utcubamba, Santa, Paucartambo.

Venezuela

Caroni, Paragua, Cama, Orinoco

Tent Versus Hammock

We are well aware that many people prefer sleeping in a hammock. We favor a tent for the following reasons:

A. A two person tent can be lighter than two comfortable hammocks.
B. It's often easier to find flat ground than two trees just the right distance apart.
C. Rigging mosquito netting over a hammock can be frustrating, whereas a tent is bug proof.

However, we completely understand the arguments in favor of hammocks, the strongest one being comfort. Did you know there's a right way and a wrong way to lie in a hammock? If you lie diagonally across it, your body and legs are more or less horizontal, not sagged into a "U" position which is uncomfortable for a whole night. And there's nothing like a siesta in a quickly set up hammock!

We have heard of jungle hammocks which sound ideal, although we've never tried them ourselves. They are a combination of a hammock, mosquito netting, and a waterproof roof, and are sometimes available from army surplus stores.

Making Your Own Tropical Tent

We've designed and made a tropical tent which has served us faithfully throughout Central and Latin America as well as Africa. It is all mosquito netting because we felt that usually bugs would be a bigger problem than rain. And you can't beat netting for a good view of the landscape, or stars, while the mosquitoes frantically whine outside. Some of our best animal viewing has been done from inside the tent!

For wet nights we use a separate cover over the netting. A lightweight tarpaulin, complete with grommets, is easily obtainable. Get it big enough to overhang front and back of the netting providing you with protection from driving rain. A tarpaulin is a great instant shelter anywhere, even in a canoe. If you're travelling in the dry season you'll be all right with two rain ponchos instead of a tarpaulin, providing they join together efficiently.

There are two disadvantages to this sort of tent: curious natives can look in at you, and the tarp flaps in the wind.

Our tent was made four years ago, and then open-mesh nylon mosquito netting was readily available. Now the craze is for very fine mesh which keeps out 'no-see-ums.' We're not sure what this material would be like in the tropics, it would probably keep out cooling breezes in addition to the bugs. Have a look at what's available locally; most good backpacking shops sell open-mesh mosquito netting in addition to the other materials you'll need.

DIRECTIONS

If you buy all the materials the right length you should end up with a two-man tent, 6'3" long, 3'9" high and 5' wide. It weighs about two pounds and will cost around $75.

YOU WILL NEED

A 13'9" length of mosquito netting, 5' wide.

Weather proof urethane-coated nylon for the floor. For the 6'3" × 5' tent you must find material only 48" wide, if you don't want a whole lot left over. If you can only buy the 5' width, you might consider reducing the width of your tent to 4'6", with a 3" rim. You can then buy just 6'9" of the material. A great financial saving. If your material is 48" wide you need to buy a 10' length.

36' Of nylon binding.

Nylon thread.

2 Double-sided zippers, one 3', one 2' long.

Aluminum tent poles for two 4' supports.

4 Aluminum tent pegs 12" long, and 8 pegs 6" long.

24' Of nylon cord, and 4 line adjusters.

In addition, you'll need a sewing machine, and a good supply of heavy duty needles. Also scissors, pins, tape measure or metal ruler,

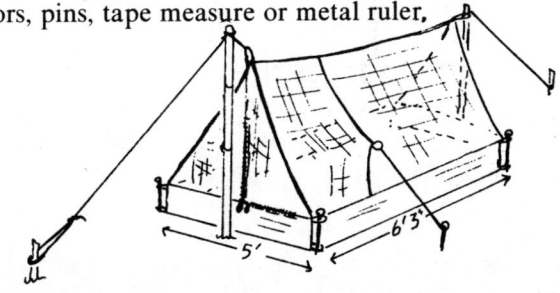

1. Make the floor to the measurements specified, sew the seam with large stitches and seal with seam sealer.

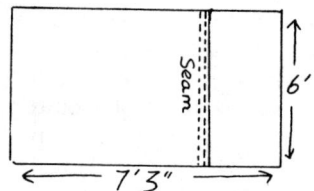

2. Turn up a six-inch rim all round by making a dart at each corner. The resulting inside 'pockets' are useful storing places for glasses, flashlight, etc.

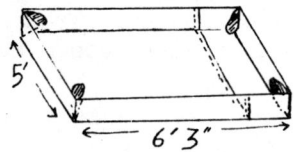

3. Cut the mosquito netting into the following lengths:
   8', 1'3", 1'3", 3'3".
   Put aside the 3'3" piece, and cut and join the others as shown. Use the nylon binding to strengthen your seam. Make loops in the binding 9" from the bottom for 'side-pulls'.

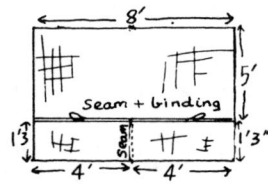

4. Sew binding along the mid-length, making loops at each end.

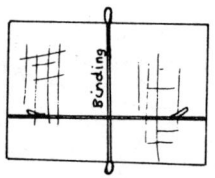

5. Sew the netting to the floor rim, and put two binding loops in each corner as shown.

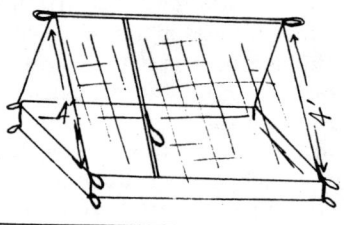

6. Divide your remaining piece of netting as shown. If you can pin it out on the floor and use a long ruler you'll be more accurate. These are the end pieces. 'A' is sewn into the back of the tent.

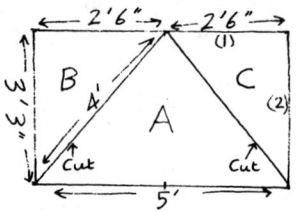

7. 'B' and 'C' are for the front opening. Sew tape round all edges, then sew the 2' zipper to side (1) and the 3' zipper to side (2) on 'C' so that both pulls meet when the zippers are closed.

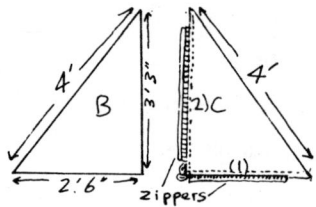

8. Sew other side of 3' zipper to 'B', and the 2' one to the bottom of the tent. Join the remaining seams.

Congratulations, you've finished your tent! Pitch it as shown in the first picture.

Building a Balsa Raft

Building a balsa raft is not an easy project, but we think it would be fun to build and try rafting. We would suggest, while gaining skill and practice, you contact locals with experience to help you build your first raft. Not only will they know which trees are the right ones, but they'll have the tools and the strength to help drag the logs to the riverbank.

The raft shown here is your basic two person model which also allows enough freeboard to keep your gear dry. For more people and equipment use more logs, longer and thicker than those shown here.

The bark must be peeled off the trunk when the tree is felled. If you can allow four or five days for your wood to dry out you'll have a higher floating, longer lasting raft.

Certain jungle vines can be used to lash the logs together, but we think it would be more practical to bring .05 cm. cord from home if you intend building a raft. Any cord left over will be gratefully received by the locals.

And don't forget your paddles, one for each person. It is difficult and time consuming to make paddles from scratch, but it is a good project for whiling away the time as your logs dry. Better still, bring collapsible aluminum paddles from home. Before setting out on your trip down the river, it would be wise to cut yourself a long, thin pole for pushing, anchoring and beating off curious caimans.

Have a great trip, and don't forget to tell us all about it.

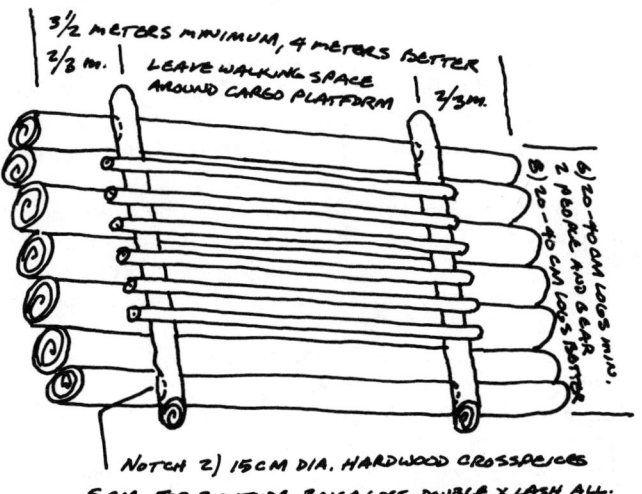

Bibliography

The number of books written about the Amazon area over the ages is hard to believe. In doing the research for this book, and compiling this bibliography, we have looked at close to a thousand library cards in four libraries. Not only is the range of subjects broad, but the detail is surprisingly deep. After all, naturalists have been visiting the area for 200 years.

The few books included in this bibliography represent only those found most credible and useful in the preparation of this book. We have omitted many titles that may be of interest to travelers only because we didn't know where to draw the line. We urge anyone interested in doing background reading to visit the nearest library or bookstore.

Guidebooks

**The South American Handbook,* edited by John Brooks, is published annually in England and is distributed in the U.S. and Canada by Rand McNally.

We wouldn't dream of traveling without it. Not only does it contain more information than any other guidebook covering Latin America, but it is particularly useful for the adventurous traveler. It is expensive, but whatever it costs it pays for itself in time, money and frustration saved.

**South America,* edited by Stephen Birnbaum, is part of a series of travel guides published by Houghton Mifflin, Boston. Penguin publishes this series in England. Not only is this guide revised annually but it is loaded with sound tips for off-the-beaten-path travelers. This is not another mainstream guidebook, it's special.

**Budget Traveler's Guide to Latin America,* edited by Marjorie Cohen, is written mainly for students. It is written under the auspices of the C.I.E.E. and is part of a series of guidebooks. Very helpful and portable with a new edition every other year. Published and distributed by E. P. Dutton, New York.

**South America on a Shoestring,* by Geoffrey Crowther, published in 1980 by Lonely Planet in Australia. Roger Lascelles distributes this title in England; Bookpeople distribute it from Berkeley; Hippocrene from New York.

**Fodor's South America,* edited by Robert Fisher, published by Fodor in New York, and by Hodder & Stoughton in London. New editions regularly.

**Exploring Cuzco,* by Peter Frost, published by Lima 2000, Lima. No, Cuzco isn't on a major river, but it is the jumping off point for several great trips. As a guide to the area this book can't be beaten for local history, where to eat, sleep and how to get around.

South America on 10–15 Dollars a Day, edited by Arnold Greenberg and published by Arthur Frommer, New York. This title, and others in the series, is distributed by Roger Lascelles, London. New editions regularly.
Myra Waldo's Travel Guide to South America, by Myra Waldo and published by Macmillan, New York. New editions regularly.
* Denotes Distributed by Bradt Enterprises, U.S.A.

Reference

International Dictionary (Spanish/English—English/Spanish; Tana de Gamez, Editor in Chief; Simon & Schuster, NY 1973.
   This is the best dictionary available with a bias toward Latin America, but is too heavy to take traveling.
Standard Encyclopedia of the World's Rivers & Lakes, Dr. R. K. Gresswell & Anthony Huxley Editors, G. P. Putnam's Sons, NY 1965.
University of Chicago Dictionary (Spanish/English—English/Spanish); Carlos Castillo & Otto Bond Compilers, Pocket Books, NY 1975.
   The best paperback dictionary to take with you to South America.
Webster's New Geographical Dictionary, G. & C. Merriam & Co., Springfield, MA 1977.
World Wildlife Guide, Viking, NY 1971. This book has a few pages on the national parks in South America and a species check list.

Natural History, Sociology, Anthropology

BATES, HENRY: *Naturalist on the River Amazon*, Dover Reprint, NY 1975.
BATES, MARSTON: *The Forest & the Sea*, Vintage Books, NY 1960. *The Land & Wildlife of South America*, Time-Life, NY 1964.
DORST, JEAN: *South & Central America: A Natural History*, Random House, NY 1967.
DUNNING, J. S.: *South American Land Birds: 1,100 Photos in Color*, Harrowood Books, Newtown Square, PA 1981.
GOODSPEAD, T. H.: *Plant Hunters*, U. of California Press, Berkeley, 1961.
MATTHIESSON, PETER: *The Cloud Forest*, Ballentine Books, NY 1961.
REICHEL-DOLMATOFF, G.: *Amazon Cosmos*, U. of Chicago Press, Chicago, 1971.
RICHARD, PAUL W.: *Tropical Rain Forest*, Cambridge U. Press, Cambridge, UK 1964.
DE SCHAUENSEE, RODOLPHE MEYER: *A Guide to the Birds of Venezuela*, Princeton University Press, NJ 1977.
   Even in paperback this book is expensive, but its plates are excel-

lent and it is well worth the money if you can find a copy.
SHOUMATOFF, ALEX: *The Rivers Amazon,* Sierra Club Books, San Francisco, 1978.
   This book contains some of the most reliable information we saw during our search, and certainly the best bibliography.
SPRUCE, RICHARD: *Notes of a Botanist on the Amazon,* Macmillan, NY 1962. Reprint.
VILLAS BOAS, CLAUDIO & ORLANDO: *Xingu: The Indians & Their Myths,* Farrar, Strauss & Giroux, NY, 1972.
   A truly wonderful book.

Periodicals

Amazonia, Orinoco & Pampas, Number 6 in the Peoples of the Earth series, published in 1973 by Robert B. Clarke, with Danbury Press, a division of Grolier Enterprises.
Americas, Pan American Union, Washington, DC 20006. Monthly.
Expedition: The Magazine of the Americas, 720—36th Ave. North, St. Petersburg, FL 33704. Bimonthly.
Globe, The Globetrotters' Club, BCM/Roving, London WC1V 6XX, England. Bi-annual.
Great Expeditions, Box 46499, Station G, Vancouver, B.C., Canada V6R 4G7. Bi-monthly.
South American Explorer, 2239 E. Cofax, Denver, CO 80206. Quarterly.
The Lima Times, Carabaya 928, Lima. Weekly.
Peru: Where, What, When, Carabaya 928, Lima. Monthly.

Fiction

MATTHIESSEN, PETER: *At Play in the Fields of the Lord,* Random House, NY 1965.
   Notable
HUDSON, WILLIAM: *Green Mansions,* a classic in many editions.
MARQUEZ, GABRIEL GARCIA: *One Hundred Years of Solitude,* Avon, NY 1977.
WILDER, THORNTON: *The Bridge of San Luis Rey.* Many editions are available of this classic.
CLEMENS, SAMUEL L.: *Life on the Mississippi.* A classic in many editions.

Index of Main Rivers and Ports

R. Amazon 62, 63, 64, 66
R. Apurímac 62-64
R. Atrato 31, 33, 52
Belém 69, 93
Benjamin Constant 69
Puerto Berrío 24, 51
R. Bio-Bio 31, 85-90
R. Cayapas 56
Coca 57, 60
R. Frio 54, 55
Coastal Waterway 24, 56, 57
Esmeraldas 56
Guajará Mirim 24, 75
Guayaramerín 75
Iquitos 24, 57, 67
Juazeiro 24, 81
Labarinto 70, 73
Leticia 21, 67
Luisiana, Hacienda 64
R. Madiera 24
R. Madre de Dios 70
R. Magdalena 24, 51
Maldanado 70, 72, 73
R. Mamoré 24, 25, 31, 75
Manaus 69, 75, 93
Manú 70-73

Misahualli 57
Mompós 51
R. Napo 57, 59
Nueva Rocafuerte 57
Pakitsa 70, 73
Pasaje 62, 64
Pirapora 81, 82
Pucallpa 24, 67, 67
Pumabamba 62, 63
Quibdó 52, 53
Ramon Castilla 67
Roroboya 21
San Lorenzo 24, 56, 57
Santerem 69
R. São Francisco 24, 31, 81
Sautatá 53
Shintuya 70, 72
Sobrado 83
Tola (La) 56
Trinidad 75, 77
Turbo 52, 53
R. Ucayali 65, 67
R. Urabamba 92
Puerto Vêlho 24
Puerto Villaroel 75

Want to do an unusual river trip in South America—or elsewhere? Need companions or information?

Let us tell you how we can help you with your ideas.

'Great Expeditions' is a membership organization for the adventurous traveler and explorer.

We have many useful services, run our own trips, have meetings throughout North America, publish 6 issues of 'Great Expeditions' newsmagazine a year, and more.

Join the adventurous explorers. For details, write: 'Great Expeditions', Box 46499, Station G, Vancouver, B.C., Canada V6R 4G7.